COVENT GARDEN AND STRAND

A History

BARRY TURNER

MENSCH PUBLISHING

Mensch Publishing
51 Northchurch Road,
London N1 4EE, United Kingdom

First published in Great Britain 2025

A catalogue record for this book is
available from the British Library

ISBN:
978-1-912914-77-7 (paperback)
978-1-912914-78-4 (ebook)

Typeset by Van-garde Imagery, Inc., • van-garde.com

Contents

Contents

Jubilee Market Traders' Plaque, Southampton Street

Preface

I came to know Covent Garden when the fruit, vegetable and flower market, the largest in Europe, was still in full swing. This was in the early 1960s. Late night student parties at the nearby London School of Economics (LSE) invariably ended up in Covent Garden where the pubs were open at all hours.

It was said of the Covent Garden of the time that it was 'a noisy, nerve-wracking place' from soon after midnight to midday when 'it fades into sleepiness and an underfoot squash of cabbage leaves and rotten apples.' Not, one might think, an appealing image. But when the Market was at its peak there were always amazing sights to be seen, not least the porters with tiers of up to a dozen baskets carried on their heads, weaving their way through narrow streets crowded with buyers and sellers.

When I was at the London School of Economics there was talk of the Market moving away from the city centre to a more spacious site. What then was to happen to the Covent Garden as we knew it? Since this was the age of the motorist who demanded the right to drive anywhere and park anywhere, political opinion favoured wholesale demolition to clear the way for traffic and pedestrian walkways.

It was not until 1974 that the Market was given a new home, three miles away at Nine Elms. Meanwhile, the original Covent Garden was left to an unholy alliance of myopic planners and venal property developers who lavished hospitality on the political decision makers. Fortunately, wiser counsel prevailed but only after a heroic fight by residents and conservationists to save the best of Covent Garden. For what might have been, look across Waterloo Bridge to the concrete jungle encompassing the National Theatre, the Hayward Gallery and the National Film Theatre, cultural gems in a dismal setting. Our Covent Garden has more appeal and, dare I say it, offers more fun. And Covent Garden has a story that marks it out as something special in London's history.

Let us begin.

1

Balthazar Nebot's 1737 painting of the square
before the 1830 market hall was constructed

The Garden Grows

*The origins of Covent Garden; Inigo Jones and the
Piazza; St Paul's, the Actors' Church; The aristocracy
and gentry move in.*

Hard though it is to imagine, there was a time about four hundred
years ago when Covent Garden, then known as Convent Garden,
was largely open pastures where sheep and cattle grazed. Part of
the land close to the village of Charing (now Charing Cross), it

provided fruit and vegetables for the wealthy Benedictine Abbey of St Peter; hence Convent Garden.

The link to the Abbey was severed when Henry VIII, appointing himself Supreme Head of the Church, decided that the lands attached to the abbeys and monasteries were rightly his, a claim backed by sufficient force to make it incontestable.

After Henry's death in 1547, the land around Long Acre, then a straggling dirt track lined by elms, was leased by the Crown to John Russell, first Earl of Bedford. With the accession of Elizabeth I, the Bedford family extended their holding but a half century was to pass before the builders moved in on the patchwork of fields and meadows. The instigator was Francis Russell, 4th Earl of Bedford, a shrewd businessman who had made his mark by heading a consortium of landowners to finance the drainage of the Cambridgeshire fens, thus creating swathes of peat-rich farmland.

Prompted by the stately houses along Strand with their gardens stretching down to the Thames, Lord Russell decided that Covent Garden was ripe for development. Targeting the well-off, who favoured fresh air over the none too salubrious aromas of the inner city, he sought royal favour for transforming Covent Garden into residences 'fit for the habitation of gentlemen and men of ability'. The consent of Charles I in return for a down payment took the project to its next critical stage, that of appointing an architect.

The front runner was Inigo Jones, surveyor to the King, whose continental travels had given him a deeper knowledge of architecture than any of his contemporaries. Taking the lead from Roman Classical and Italian Renaissance design, the lasting testimony to his genius is the Queen's House at Greenwich and the Banqueting House in Whitehall. If Inigo Jones had a fault it was extravagance, a throwback to his early days as the producer of lavish court entertainments known as masques. Combining music, dancing, singing and acting with a cast of hundreds, a masque required an elaborate stage design with no expense spared. Lord Russell was made of sterner stuff. While he was committed to 'buildings that would serve to ornament the town' his brief to Inigo Jones was to blend creativity with economy.

Inspired by the piazzas in the Tuscan seaport of Livorno and the Place des Vosges in Paris, Inigo Jones came up with a plan for an open square with terraced houses built of brick (a rarity at the time) on three sides with the fourth side occupied by a church dedicated to St Paul. The houses facing the square had front doors opening onto an arcade intended for bystanders and strollers.

Covent Garden Piazza introduced London to town planning, a radical concept that stood in contrast to the piecemeal spread of crooked, narrow streets and thrown-together half-timbered houses that typified the old City. The handsomely designed garden square was to become standard for upper class London though, contrary to Inigo's vision, the open spaces were generally reserved exclusively for residents.

While impressed by the overall design, Lord Russell balked at the cost. Trimming the budget required the sacrifice of the houses on the south side of the square where the garden of Bedford

3

House (now Southampton Street) was sectioned off by a high wall. Even so, Inigo Jones earned high praise. Richard Brome, a popular writer of topical comedies introduced 'the great builder' into one of his plays, declaiming how 'the master of his great art... has wedded strength to beauty...commodiousness with perspicuity!' concluding 'All, all is as't should be'.

Though little now remains of Inigo's imaginative concept for refined living, St Paul's Church, the first to be built in almost a century, remains an outstanding example of his work. As told by the waspish Horace Walpole, no friend of classical design but rather a disciple of what might be described as Gothic Grotesque, Lord Russell wanted a place of worship 'not much better than a barn'. The response from the architect was to promise 'the handsomest barn in England'. And, this is precisely what he achieved.

Nothing if not commodious, St Paul's nonetheless radiates friendly intimacy. In his *Critical Review of Buildings*, Benjamin Ralph, writing in 1783, described St Paul's as 'one of the most perfect pieces of architecture that art of man can produce' while John Wesley, who preached here, judged St Paul's to be the 'longest and best constructed parish church'.

A curiosity of St Paul's is the portico facing the Piazza. Intended as the front entrance, it incurred the opposition of Church dignitaries who insisted that it was the altar not the approach that had to be placed at the east end of the building. Short of starting afresh, Inigo sealed off the portico in favour of a new entrance via the churchyard at the rear. Long since closed for burials, St Paul's is now entered through an attractive garden, the only green space left in Covent Garden.

Ecclesiastically speaking, St Paul's had a shaky start. Completed in 1633 it was not consecrated until 1638. The delay was caused by a dispute with the vicar of nearby St Martin's-in-the-Fields, then a small church bearing no resemblance to the handsome structure we see today, who claimed Covent Garden and St Paul's as part of his parish. This was vigorously denied by Lord Russell who, after all, had provided the site and paid for the construction. It took over twenty years for the demarcation to be finally resolved in favour of Covent Garden.

Known as the Actors' Church for the number of christenings, wedding, funerals and services related to the drama, St Paul's boasts a profusion of memorial tablets to departed stars of stage and screen and to those who provided the means for their success.

One of the early plaques commemorates Thomas Arne who wrote music for plays, masques and pantomimes. He was born in Covent Garden in 1710 and for many years lived at 31 King Street. His father, an upholsterer and undertaker, had little time for his son's musical ambitions but failed to dampen his spirit. At night when most of the family was asleep, Thomas practised on his spinet, muffling the sound with a cloth. He is now best known for *Rule Britannia*, written for a masque performed before Frederick Prince of Wales, son of George II. This rousing song, extolling the virtues of Britain and its Empire, became a favourite for royal occasions. Two hundred years later, at the official opening of the Royal Festival Hall on the Thames South Bank, George

VI, whose musical appreciation did not extend much beyond the National Anthem, was so enthused by Sir Malcolm Sargent's boisterous version of *Rule Britannia* for soloist, chorus and state trumpeters and full orchestra, that he led the audiences in a standing ovation. At a reception afterwards, the King told Sargent that *Rule Britannia* should be played at every concert. Sargent tactfully pointed out that it might not always be appropriate. 'In that case', declared the King, 'I won't be there'. Today *Rule Britannia* is still heard at the annual last night of the Proms at the Albert Hall, though its archaic sentiments are thought by many to be inappropriate for community singing. Arne's less controversial *A-Hunting We Will Go*, composed for a production of *The Beggar's Opera*, has lasted as a popular folk song.

A more rumbustious character with a tablet in St Paul's is the eighteenth century actor and dramatist, Charles Macklin. Credited with a natural style of acting as opposed to the declamatory mode favoured by players who stepped out of their roles to deliver their big speeches face on to the audience, Macklin made his name with his portrayal of Sherlock in *A Merchant of Venice*. Those who saw his performance recognised, for the first time, a real person rather than the ludicrously comic Shylock as usually portrayed.

Often in trouble for his foul temper, Macklin faced a charge of murder after stabbing a fellow actor in the eye with a stage dagger. Conducting his own defence, he managed to persuade the court to accept his plea of manslaughter. Whatever his faults, Macklin was undoubtedly a trouper. At age 86, he appeared on stage as Macbeth, prompting a critic to observe that 'if there was anything to praise in the performance it was the foolhardy presumption of Macklin in daring to take on the role'.

Macklin's tablet in St Paul's, showing a dagger piercing a theatrical mask, a clear reference to his infamous transgression, gives his age as 107. But as so much in his life, this was short of the truth. Even so, if, realistically, ten years is deducted from his span, it was not a bad innings for one who lived life dangerously and to the full.

St Paul's in the eighteenth century was a rich source of gossip, never more fruitful than in 1764 when Lady Susan Strangeways, daughter of the Earl of Ilchester, escaped the family clutches to marry a Mr O'Brien, a penniless young actor who compensated for his poverty with seductive powers. Since Lady Susan had lately celebrated her coming of age, the nuptials could not be challenged. Horace Walpole, who disapproved of actors on principle, recorded his sympathy for the father of the bride. 'Indeed, it is the completion of disgrace – even a footman were preferable; the publicity of the hero's profession perpetuates the mortification...I could not have believed that Lady Susan would have stooped so low.' But Lady Susan had her champions. A broad-minded peer who met her after her marriage, confessed to be 'quite enchanted' with Lady Susan O'Brien as she now was.

St Paul's was gutted by fire in 1795 with only the walls and portico escaping the flames. Fastening the blame was all the more contentious after it was found that the insurance policy had been allowed to lapse. The cost of rebuilding in the original style was met by an increase in the ground rents on Covent Garden premises.

Latterly the backdrop for street entertainers, the portico of St Paul's has achieved lasting theatre and movie fame as the setting for the first encounter of Professor Higgins with the flower girl Eliza Doolittle in G.B.Shaw's *Pygmalion* and its musical spin-off *My Fair Lady*.

Among the street performers seen recently was a Charlie Chaplin lookalike complete with battered hat, clipped moustache and a bendy cane that he waved in time with his jaunty walk. Did he know, one wonders, that Charlie Chaplin himself made a brief appearance as a Covent Garden entertainer? This was in 1902 when, as a thirteen-year-old, scraping a living, the soon to be great comedian helped shell a delivery of walnuts. As a reward he was given a ticket to a music hall where the popular Walford Bodie, magician, ventriloquist and hypnotist, was topping the bill. Adopting the dramatic gestures that were a big part of Bodie's performance, Chaplin busked an easily recognisable imitation of the stage entertainer. Grateful for the pennies collected, he must have dreamt of better times.

To return to the early days of Covent Garden, its status as a prime residential district was much enhanced by two catastrophes suffered by the City of London. The first was the 1665 Plague which ravaged the tightly confined and polluted living quarters. In late August, the diarist Samuel Pepys recorded:

Every day sadder and sadder news. In the City died this week 7,496; and of them 6,102 of the plague. But it is feared that the true number of the dead this week is nearer 10,000

*– partly from the poor that cannot be taken notice of through
the greatness of the number, and partly from the Quakers
and others that will not have any bell ring for them.*

In all, the Plague exterminated up to 100,000 citizens, up to a fifth of London's total population.

A year later came the Great Fire. John Evelyn witnessed the terrible scene:

*The conflagration was so universal, and the people so
astonish'd, that from the beginning, I know not by what
despondency or fate, they hardly stirr'd to quench it...All
the skie was of a fiery aspect, like the top of a burning
oven, and the light seene above 40 miles round about
for many nights.*

Small wonder that those with the means fastened on to Covent Garden as a haven. Ever the social climber, Samuel Pepys made note of his visit to one of the more prominent residences flanking the Piazza:

*I was with my Lord Brouncker and Mrs Williams by
coach with four horses to London, to my Lord's house in
Covent Garden, But Lord! What staring to see a noble-
man's coach come to town! And porters everywhere bow
to us; and such begging of beggars!*

Evidence that the gentry was making the running appears in the parish records of St Paul's Church where details were recorded of those renting out pews, a widespread source of church income until well into the nineteenth century.

In 1690 the Rt Hon. Edward Russell, treasurer of the Navy, took over the pew belonging to the lord bishop of Durham who had left the area. In 1694, the Rt Hon. Robert Lord Russell paid six guineas for a number nine pew on the wall side of the north aisle, and he was also allowed to make a door in the north wall to the pew. The following year Henry Strudwick asked that himself and his wife might be seated in the great pew in the south side of the 'middle isle'. He paid £5.

2

Cora Pearl, aged 29, and Prince Achille Murat (1865)

High Life, Low Life

A new cultural network of artists and writers; Coffee houses and gin palaces; Courtesans and prostitutes; Crime and detection.

In 1700 historian John Strype declared Covent Garden to be 'well inhabited by a mixture of nobility, gentry and wealthy tradesmen'. That social structure was soon to change. Favouring more spacious surroundings the nobility moved to palatial houses in Piccadilly and Mayfair leaving Covent Garden to writers, artists and actors who felt at home in the coffee houses and taverns that were springing up around the Piazza. With the demolition of Bedford House in 1705, the whole area of what today we recognise as Covent Garden was leased out by the Bedford Estate for speculative building. A new cultural network began to take shape.

Fencing Master Henry Angelo recalled Covent Garden as 'the residence of a succession of men renowned for genius, talent, wit, humour and eccentricity'. In 1764 the Piazza boasted ten or more well-known artists including Richard Wilson, the father of landscape painting, Sir James Thornhill with his academy for nude studies and scene painter and landscape artist, George Lambert.

Widely praised for their portrayal of royal favourites though less well-regarded today, Sir Peter Lely and Sir Godfrey Kneller had studios by the Piazza. The German born Kneller came to be employed in royal circles starting with Charles II and continuing through the reigns of James II, William III and Queen Anne. A prolific painter, albeit with the help of numerous assistants, Kneller made a large fortune and was, by all accounts, a crashing bore who, like all bores, took himself far too seriously. A poet who exercised his wit to devastating effect, Alexander Pope could not resist teasing Kneller. Well aware, as he put it, that no flattery was so gross but that Kneller would not swallow it, he proved his point by enlisting God's help. 'I believe if the Almighty had had your assistance', he told Sir Godfrey, 'the world would have been formed more perfect'. Said Kneller, 'Fore God, I believe so'. Arrogant though he was, Kneller was a shrewd businessman. To save time and effort, he sketched only the faces of the society ladies who sat for him. Their body and hands were those of his housemaid.

Johan Zoffany, famed for his theatre paintings, endured hard times in a Drury Lane garret. Born in Germany where his father was architect to the Prince of Thurn and Taxis. At aged 16, Johan left home to travel to Rome. In 1760 he arrived in London where his wife of three years left him. The celebrated clockmaker Stephen Rimbault, based in Seven Dials, came to his rescue paying him enough for his clock paintings to survive until he was taken up by actor David Garrick who sat for him in several of his leading roles. Thereafter, his success was assured.

Grinling Gibbons, one of the greatest wood carvers of his or any generation, lived in Bow Street. Examples of his exquisite craftsmanship can be seen in St Paul's Church where he is buried.

By far the greatest artist nurtured by Covent Garden was J,M.W. Turner who might justifiably be regarded as the first impressionist. He was born in April 1775 at 26 Maiden Lane where his father, William Turner, was a hairdresser and wig maker and where the young William's first paintings were displayed for sale in his shop window. His premises were well chosen. As a residential district for people of quality, Covent Garden was a mecca for the latest fashions. Young aristocrats returning from their Grand

Tours of the Continent adopted the style of the French court which favoured elaborate, ponderous wigs, often coloured, with long cascading curls.

It was an expensive indulgence and William Turner, who was a skilled practitioner and much liked by his patrons who found him an engaging character, thrived on it. Even after the wealthiest families had moved on, the modish young bucks chose to show off their sartorial splendour in the cultured milieu that was fast taking over in Covent Garden.

Maiden Lane was at the heart of intellectual ferment with its booksellers, bookbinders, engravers and printers. Directly above Turner's place of business was John Moreing's Great Auction Rooms where the young Turner could feast his eyes on works of art, mostly old master paintings that were up for sale, this at a time when there were no public galleries of any note. Nor for that matter, were there any schools or academies for training artists. This began to change in the mid-eighteenth century. In 1754 at Rawthmell's Coffee House in Henrietta Street, a gathering of artists and art teachers founded a Society for the Encouragement of Arts, Manufacturers and Commerce soon to be better known as the Society of Arts and today as the Royal Society of Arts (RSA). The objective was to encourage collaboration between art and commerce and to stimulate innovation.

In 1760 a Society of Artists was set up to mount an annual exhibition of British contemporary art, an initiative that attracted a daily attendance of up to one thousand. The Society also set up a drawing and painting school. A breakaway group calling itself the

Royal Academy of Arts settled for a time in Somerset House, a new set of public buildings on Strand, moving in 1837 to Trafalgar Square where it shared space with the National Gallery, before finally changing its address to Burlington House on Piccadilly where it remains today.

Encouraged by his father who recognised a latent talent, young William Turner was swept along on this aesthetic tide. Some of his earliest drawings were of objects in the showroom of Humphrey Tomkinson, a gold and silver smith who lived in Maiden Lane and was one of Turner Senior's clients. Inspiration was closer to home in his father's busy shop with its magnificently attired clients and the phantasmagoria of bright colours.

But Covent Garden had its drawbacks. For young people of less than robust constitution, a category that included the ten-year-old William, the threat of contagious disease was very real. After the death of a younger sister reinforced the risk, William was sent to live with his uncle Joseph Marshall whose home was in Brentwood, then a small market town.

But if William was ever homesick for the excitement of Covent Garden he was more than compensated by his friend-ship with the two young sons of Sarah Trimmer a campaigning educationist, landscape painter and daughter of Joshua Kirby, one-time president of the Society of Artists. Turner's latest biographer, Franny Moyle suggests, convincingly, that William was influenced by Sarah Trimmer's *Easy Introduction to the Knowledge of Nature* to explore the rural landscape and wildlife that gave a new dimension to his drawing. Many of these topographical views found their way back to his father's shop where they were put on prominent display for sale to customers and stall holders along Maiden Lane which, incidentally, was never as demure as its name suggests. The likely derivation of Maiden is a corruption of 'midden', a rubbish or dung heap.

The origins of the fruit and vegetable market date from the time when the houses flanking the Piazza were first occupied. Where there was money tradesmen were soon to be found although initially their numbers were tightly controlled. The Great Fire of 1666 which destroyed the inner City street market, led to the creation of a licensed market in Covent Garden 'well served with choice goods' to be held on the Piazza on Tuesdays, Thursdays and Saturdays.

Produce from the market gardens that lined the Thames from Greenwich to Brentford was brought in by river barges or pack horses and wagons drawn by six or more horses. Barges were unloaded at wharves below Strand where porters were on hand to carry the freight up the hill to the market. For the return journey, the barges carried manure and street sweepings to serve as fertiliser.

Cabbages, carrots, onions, leeks and garlic were piled high though potatoes were still regarded as a luxury. Lettuce was thought of more as a medicine than as a vegetable, taken with salt and oil it was said to cool the blood and act as a sedative. Of the variety of apples on sale, one of the most popular was the large custard which gave its name to the costermongers who manned the barrows or stalls. More exotic fruits such as peaches and apricots were rumoured to be dangerous to health while even the humble tomato was thought to cause cancer as well as being an aphrodisiac. The cucumber was another suspect vegetable. In August 1663, Pepys noted 'Mr Newbourne is dead of eating cucumbers'. Asparagus, on the other hand, was hugely popular, as too was watercress, gathered wild and sold in bundles.

As the market expanded, it was the 5th Earl of Bedford, soon to be raised to a dukedom, the pinnacle of British aristocracy, who reckoned on improving his finances by putting the market on a more regular footing. To prepare the way he persuaded Charles II to grant him the right to hold a market for fruit, vegetables, herbs and other produce in a place 'commonly called the Piazza, near the Church of St Paul...every day of the week except Sundays and the Feast of the Nativity of Our Lord'. This was in 1670 by which time there were already several shops and stalls built up against the garden wall of Bedford House. But free enterprise was constrained by rules imposed by the Earl. The market was to be held within the rails that marked off the Piazza. The frontage of the new shops had to be one foot lower than the garden wall, a freeway had to be left between the shops and the rails to allow for carriages and carts, and the whole place had to be kept clean and in good repair; a noble sentiment that was all but impossible to enforce. The customer base for itinerant traders expanded with new thoroughfares linking in to the Piazza such as Henrietta Street named after Henrietta Maria, wife of Charles I, King Street, James Street and Russell Street.

Further afield, St Martin's Lane, marking the western boundary of Covent Garden, took shape with houses that offered a mix of rural and urban amenities. A vine nearly a hundred feet long, produced an annual 'pipe (720 bottles) of wine'.

At 60 St Martin's Lane, Thomas Chippendale had his workshop. The foremost furniture designer and maker of his day, Chippendale's reputation was founded on a catalogue of designs entitled *The Gentleman and Cabinet Makers' Directory* published in 1754. Accepted as the arbiter of good taste, Chippendale attracted commissions from the newly rich merchant class, many of whom lived in and around Covent Garden. While the name of Chippendale became synonymous with quality, to describe a chair or cabinet as Chippendale covered a variety of styles, albeit nearly always crafted in mahogany. The Chippendale family business remained in St Martin's Lane until 1813 when Thomas Chippendale's son, also named Thomas, was declared a bankrupt and evicted.

To turn to literary affairs, it was in a back parlour of a bookshop in Russell Street that James Boswell first met Dr Johnson. Boswell, who was to become Johnson's amanuensis and biographer, recorded their encounter in his diary for May 16, 1763:

Mr Johnson is a man of a most dreadful appearance. He is a very big man, is troubled with sore eyes, the palsy and the king's evil. He is very slovenly in his dress and speaks with a most uncouth voice. Yet his knowledge and strength of expression command vast respect and render

him very excellent company. He has great humour and is
a worthy man. But his dogmatical roughness of manners is
disagreeable.

Despite the reservations, Boswell found in Johnson an intellect worthy of dog-like devotion.

Of the other literary greats, Samuel Taylor Coleridge lived for three years in King Street writing political pieces for the *Morning Post*. Washington Irving, the first American writer to win acclaim in Europe, shared lodgings at 22 Henrietta Street. It was at a tavern, the Bedford Head, in Maiden Lane that Voltaire, the arch opponent of religious intolerance and persecution, lodged between 1726 and 1729. He learnt English by reading the *Spectator* and attending the plays at Drury Lane where he used a written text to help him follow what was being said on stage. Brought up on Sophocles and Racine, Voltaire had never even heard of Shakespeare when he first arrived in London. When one day he was jeered as a 'French dog' he promptly stood on a boundary stone and addressed the mob like Mark Antony, 'My fine Englishmen, am I not already wretched enough that I was not born one of ye?' His eloquence saved him from a beating.

Thomas De Quincey slowly poisoned himself on opium at 36 Tavistock Street where he lived from 1785 to 1809 and where he wrote his classic *Confessions of an Opium Eater*. It is a curiosity that the Victorian obsession with a narrowly defined morality did not extend to drugs. There were doctors who recommended opium as 'a sage and noble panacea'. Elizabeth Bennett was among the intellectual elite who praised De Quincey as a writer who 'vivifies words, or deepens them and gives them profound significance'. As his biographer Frances Wilson explains: 'by simulating the experience of an opium dream, he presented the Victorians with a performance of High Romanticism fuelled by spontaneous overflows of powerful feeling, longings for the infinite and unbounded, fearless descents into the childhood imagination, and a deep knowledge of the numinous'.

Coffee houses proliferated after the merchant ships of the East India Company introduced London to this flavoursome and stimulating beverage. In the best establishments, 'you had a dish of coffee, a good fire to sit by, the chance to meet your friends, discuss business and politics and, above all, read the newspapers'.

It is easy to dismiss the coffee houses as haunts for idlers who had nothing better to do with their time. This is to ignore the social context in which the coffee houses thrived. For this was the age of the Enlightenment when the traditional monopoly of aristocratic privilege was challenged by scientific discoveries and rational argument. The coffee house was the meeting place for educated men to discuss the topics of the day. These deliberations filtered through to public policy on such as religious toleration and individual liberty.

The reputable coffee houses in Covent Garden were Will's, Button's and Tom's, all in Russell Street also known for its smart shops. It was at Will's that Dryden held court in the place of honour 'by the fire in winter and on the balcony in summer'. The foremost poet of his generation, Dryden in conversation was valued for his wit and for his sharp observations on the cultural scene. Such was his fame, that he earned a place in Macaulay's majestic *History of England*:

> *The great press was to get near the chair where John Dryden sat. To bow to the Laureate and to hear his opinions of Racine's latest tragedy, or of Bossu's treatise on epic poetry, was thought to be a privilege.*

Away from his peers there were those who found Dryden arrogant and pompous. Jonathan Swift (*Gulliver's Travels*) declared the conversation at Will's, invariably with Dryden at the centre, to be 'the worst...I have ever heard in my life'. Another antagonist was the Earl of Rochester, a poet of equal merit to Dryden, if less productive. Rumbustious and licentious, Rochester was the opposite of Dryden who put store by convention and respectability. Of Rochester he wrote:

> *Mean in every action, lewd in every limb,*
> *Manners themselves are mischievous to him;*
> *A glass he gives to very foul design*
> *And one must own his very vices shine.*

On a late evening in December 1679, after leaving Will's, Dryden was brutally attacked on his way to his lodgings in Long Acre. It was quickly assumed by Dryden's friends and by Dryden himself, that Rochester was responsible. As his latest biographer, Alexander Larman leaves the question hanging while pointing out that by the time of the assault Rochester was so weakened by the advanced stages of syphilis he had neither the strength nor the inclination to take vengeance on his severest critic.

Opposite Will's on Russell Street was Button's, favoured by Joseph Addison and Sir Richard Steele, journalist pamphleteers and founders of *The Tatler*, *Spectator* and the short-lived *Guardian* (not to be confused with the present-day *Guardian*), who depended for their material on coffee house discourse. Distancing themselves from religious and political factions, Addison and Steele set the standard for quality journalism. Their aim was to spread knowledge and to encourage civilised debate on contentious issues. Good humour was the mark of their publications. So much at home were they at Button's that a letter box, shaped as a lion's head, was fixed to the door for contributors to drop off their copy. 'The head is to open a most wide and voracious mouth which will then take in such letters and papers as are conveyed to me by my correspondents', declared Addison, adding 'Whatever the lion swallows I shall digest for the use of the public...I intend to make him roar so loud as to be heard all over the British nation'. In 1750, the lion's head letter box was removed to the nearby *Shakespeare Tavern* and after several other moves ended up at Woburn Abbey, the country estate of the Bedford family.

On the same street as Button's was Tom's, a favourite meeting place for Oliver Goldsmith and Dr Johnson. Customers were expected to be smartly dressed and well mannered. Tom's was one of several coffee house to be transformed into a club. Around seven hundred members paid an annual guinea subscription. Other coffee houses were less salubrious. In one of them, knives and forks were chained to the tables.

Holding first place for notoriety was Tom King's (not to be confused with Tom's) on the Piazza where more than coffee was on offer. King was a rakish old Etonian who used his social connections to attract business. It was not until his early death, brought on by fast living, when his widow Moll took over the management that the place really began to hum.

In contrast to her husband, Moll was of humble origins; her father, an alcoholic cobbler, while her mother sold fruit and vegetables on the Piazza. After a brief period as a housemaid, Moll hired a barrow to sell nuts, an enterprise that enabled her to build her savings. Her marriage to Tom, in 1717, was conducted by an unfrocked clergyman, one of many who, despite the obvious impediment, were authorised to perform the ceremony. After a rocky start when Tom was easily distracted by the Covent Garden ladies of easy virtue, the couple settled their differences by opening a coffee house in what was little more than a two-storey shed against the old wall of Bedford House.

At Moll King's', says the writer of *Odds and Ends About Covent Garden*, 'might be found the bucks, bloods, demireps, and choice spirits of London, associated with the most elegant and fascinating Cyprians (prostitutes), congregated with every species of human kind that intemperance, idleness, necessity, or curiosity, could assemble together.'

Moll took care to avoid charges of keeping a brothel. No beds were provided, assignations had to be consummated off the premises. William Hogarth was a frequent visitor, the revellers inspiring his 'modern, moral subjects' such as *A Harlot's Progress* and *A Rake's Progress*.

If Moll had a virtue, it was her ability to stay sober while all around her were sloshed out of their minds. Nonetheless, in 1739 she was sentenced to three months in Newgate for keeping a disorderly house. Though she bounced back, her coffee house, now known as Moll King's, lost all semblance of respectability, becoming 'the haunt of every kind of 'virtuperance, idleness and the eccentric'. Moll was dubbed the Fat Princess, 'inviting all to join her Bacchanalian rites'. Six years later she retired to her villa on Haverstock Hill where she had invested in a row of houses known as Moll King's Row. A convert to church-going, she was noted for her generosity to women on the breadline.

That managing a coffee house returned a good living was evidenced by George Carpenter, a Covent Garden porter renowned for carrying fifteen baskets on his head, who turned his hand to dispensing, according to William Hickey, 'a Spartan mixture, difficult to ascertain the ingredients of, but which served as coffee'. Carpenter's Coffee House was also known as the Finish since it was the place to finish up when there was nowhere else to go after a night out.

Some place that's like the FINISH, lads
Where all your high pedestrian pads
That have been up and out all night,
Running their rigs among the rattlers,
At morning meet, and – honour bright, -
Agree to share the blunt and tatlers.

'Rigs among the rattlers' was robbing travellers in chaises; 'blunt and tatlers' were money and watches.

George Carpenter was succeeded by Mother Butler, dubbed the Queen of Covent Garden, who was said to be 'witty, generous-hearted and a very extraordinary woman'. At the Finish, under her rule, 'you may take shelter till morning, very often in the *very best* of company'. Of the odd characters employed by the Finish, the oddest was a potboy called Shooter who made friends of the cellar rats by feeding them dregs of beer. 'The rats grew so fond of him that they would creep all over him and he used to carry them between his shirt and waistcoat and call them by their names'.

With the expansion of the Market the genteel attractions of Covent Garden came under threat. While there were still well-to-do families in such as King Street, elsewhere homes were divided and sub-divided to provide cheap lodgings. Seven Dials, with its Doric column as the meeting of six rather than seven streets, grew to be one of the worst slums in London, its economy based on casual labour in the Market, drinking dens and brothels.

In the smarter quarters, residents complained of the incessant cries of the costermongers proclaiming at the tops of their voices that the produce on their stalls was the best and cheapest on offer. Beloved of children, the muffin man announced his presence on the Piazza by ringing a hand bell. Such was his popularity, he was celebrated in the nonsense nursery rhyme:

Oh, who has seen the muffin-man,
The muffin-man, the muffin-man?
Has anybody seen the muffin-man

Who lives in Crumpet Lane?

On market days, wagons and carts clogged the thoroughfares making it a challenge for pedestrians trying to push through. An appeal to the magistrates in June 1731 on behalf of respectable residents and shopkeepers complained of 'Several persons of most notorious character and infamous wicked lives...have taken up residence...mainly in the neighbourhood of Drury Lane which is infected with such vile people that there are frequent outcries of the night, fighting and robberies and all sorts of debauchings'.

As far as one can tell, little was done to pacify the complainants. In 1748, the church wardens of St Paul's were moved to deliver a protest to the Duke of Bedford.

> *The Market contrary to original usage has for many*
> *years abounded with diverse ranges of sheds shops*
> *and stalls many of which have been erected since the*
> *commencement of the present lease wherein several*
> *trades or occupations of sundry sorts are carried on and*
> *exercised and which could never have been intended*
> *by your Grace to be permitted in an Herb-Market*
> *such as Covent Garden originally was...with bakers,*
> *haberdashers, cook shops, retailers of Geneva and other*
> *spirituous liquors and sundry other traders to the great*
> *annoyance and prejudice of several tradesmen of the said*
> *Parish who pay large rents.*

But, the tide of commerce, however dubious, was not to be held back.

If coffee houses and taverns could be unruly, they were models of rectitude compared to the gin palaces of Drury Lane. Their brightly lit exteriors, all plate glass and gilt cornices, were given added enticement by the promise of exotic refreshments within. A hostelry offering 'The only real brandy in London' was rivalled only by a near neighbour selling 'The famous cordial, medicated gin, which is so strongly recommended by the faculty'. The gin palaces were at their busiest on Saturday nights after the week's wages had been collected. Max Schlesinger in his *Saunterings In and About London* (1835) recorded that:

> *A dense fog, with a deep red colouring, from the reflections of numberless gas-jets, and the pavement flooded with mud, gave fitful illumination according to the strength of the gas, which flares forth in long jets…If your nerves are delicate, you had better not pass too close by the gin-shops for as the door opens – and those doors are always opening – you are overwhelmed with the pestilential fumes of gin. The pavements are crowded. Slatternly servants with baskets hurry to the butchers and grocers, and the haunters of the coffee-houses of Drury-lane elbow their way through the very midst of the population – the sweepings of humanity. A wicked world this, but the only one fit for these forms of woe*

and livid faces, in which hunger contends with thirst,
and vice with disease.

Drury Lane was the centre of a thriving sex industry. The sign of a bunch of grapes or a woman's arm indicated a brothel of which there were many. On the south east side of the market was Hummums, an all-night Turkish bath or bagnio catering for all proclivities.

There were periods when Hummums aimed at respectability. In 1701, a new management pledged to rectify 'all those neglects and abuses that were formerly done here' while offering facilities 'where persons may sweat and bathe in the cleanliest.' After Hummums burned down in 1769, it was rebuilt as a hotel.

Of famous disrepute was Betty Careless's bagnio in Tavistock Row, the subject of Hogarth's last print in the sequence of the Rake's Progress. Betty, herself a renowned beauty, made a fortune from her girls but spent too freely and died in poverty. But not entirely without regrets. *The Gentleman's Magazine* paid tribute to her skill in 'helping gay gentlemen of this country to squander £50,000'.

More successful in holding on to her money was Mother Jane Douglas who kept a milliner's shop on the corner of Russell Street where her business of a more dubious kind was conducted behind a screen of demure, if scantily dressed young ladies, working away with their needles. Mother Douglas prided herself on providing clients with services that went beyond the carnal to include excellent food and wine. Though for most part she managed to keep on the right side of the law, Mother Douglas incurred the wrath of distinguished men who felt slighted by her lack of respect. Describing her house as a 'cattery', Sir Charles Hanbury Williams said of Mother Douglas that she was 'a great flabby, stinking, swearing, hollowing, ranting Billingsgate Bawd', though he had to concede that she had once been a slender, genteel beauty. A reformed character in her later years, Mother Douglas became an ardent church-goer.

Sir John Fielding who, as chief magistrate at Bow Street, was to play a pivotal role in bringing a semblance of law and order to Covent Garden, was inclined to the view that 'all the prostitutes in the kingdom had picked up (the Piazza) as their rendez-vous.' Given the profusion of taverns, gambling dens and brothels it was a pardonable exaggeration.

Those in search of a cheap thrill were not short of pointers. In his exhaustive memoir, William Hickey recalled roaming Covent Garden with his friends after dark. At Wetherby's, a drinking den off Drury Lane, they were checked out by 'a cut-throat looking rascal' peering at them through a small wicket before opening the door. They were greeted with the spectacle of two half-naked, bleeding, and wholly drunken, women having a wrestling match:

> *For several minutes not a creature interfered between*
> *them, or seemed to care a straw what mischief they*
> *might do each other, and the contest went on with*
> *unabated fury.*

In another corner, a muscular young man was being attacked by:

*Three Amazonian tigresses who were pummelling him
with their might, aided by men armed with sticks. The
central figure retaliated to the best of his considerable
ability, knocking each assailant down with his fists
whenever the opportunity offered and whether it as a
woman or a man.'*

That much of this was play acting dawned on Hickey some weeks
later when he recognised the two violent lady wrestlers chatting
together as the best of friends.

In 1761 appeared the first edition of *Harris's List of Covent
Garden Ladies*, an alarmingly frank guide to the prostitutes who
made Covent Garden their pitch. Specialist services were noted
along with clients' rankings.

*Poll Johnson. Russell Street, Covent Garden. A delicate
plump girl who has various prices from ten shillings to
Five Guineas according to the pocket of the Cull. Her
principal trade is with Petty Officers, some of whom have
paid handsomely for their frolics.*

*Miss Bird alias Johnson. Brydges St, Covent Garden.
A tall, thin genteel girl agreeable in her manners...seen
every night at the Ben Jonsons Head. She has a northern
brogue and is too often in a state of intoxication.*

*Poll Talbot. Bow Street. Covent Garden. A fair, comely
Dame who by long intercourse...has learnt that the
profession of a Purveyor is more profitable than that of a*

Private Trader, and for that reason has opened a House
for amusement of genteel Company where Gentlemen
and Ladies will meet with a Civil Reception. She loves
the smack of the Whip sometimes...

A prosperous Covent Garden pimp, Harris promoted him-self as a public benefactor, claiming that prostitution contributed to 'the peace of families, of cities, nay, of kingdoms'. No mention was made of abuse against women and only passing reference to sexually transmitted diseases. Published and updated annually, *Harris's Guide* enjoyed a thirty-eight year run.

Of the few women who thrived on promiscuity while hold-ing to their independence, the torch bearer was Eliza Emma Crouch, known to posterity as Cora Pearl. Daughter of a finan-cially stretched Plymouth music teacher and composer who aban-doned his family to make a new life in Canada, Eliza was sent to a convent school in Boulogne. Here she remained for eight years, learning French while retaining her Cockney accent.

Returning to Britain, she lived with her grandmother in London where, as a buxom twenty-year-old, she was seduced by a middle-aged diamond merchant who took her to a low bar in Covent Garden. At least, that was her story. In any event, hav-ing taken lodgings in Covent Garden, she perfected her image as an alluring woman about town. With her sumptuous curves, dyed hair, painted eyelashes and face powders tinted with silver and pearl, she captivated a string of rich lovers. Departing for Paris, where she was famous for her loud vulgarity, Cora charmed her way into the court of Emperor Napoleon III. Her lovers included the Prince of Orange, heir to the Dutch throne, the Duc de Morny, Napoleon's half-brother, and the Emperor himself. Showered with expensive gifts, she was said to 'look like a jeweller's window'. As one of the most celebrated courtesans in Paris, Cora lived in style in a chateau on the banks of the Loiret, where she had her own chef and entertained extravagantly.

To enliven one of her dinner parties she promised to serve meat which none of her guests would dare to cut. The delectable dish turned out to be Cora herself, naked on a huge silver platter, her modesty camouflaged by a sprinkling of parsley. Appearing as Eve at a fancy-dress ball, an English journalist noted that 'her form and figure were not concealed by any more garments than were worn by the original apple-eater'. When she took to the stage it was as Cupid in Offenbach's comic opera *Orphée aux Enfers*. The cream of Parisian male society turned out to hear her sing *I Know Love*. One of the young ladies of the chorus recalled:

> *All Paris was there to see and hear when she made her appearance in the scene on Olympus. A crown of roses was on her head, and her costume consisted of a short gauze tunic, very décolleté. When she began the well-known verses, with a strong English accent,*
>
> *'Je sois Kioupidonne, mon amor*
> *Ah fait l'école bouissonière...'*

*The noise was deafening, and drowned all further
words. While the smart set applauded frantically, a
number of students in the galleries, who had come
to protest against 'la morale outrage' and 'imperial
corruption', began whistling and hooting. Cora replied
by putting out her tongue and sneering at them. This
went on every night for a week, the noise being heard
outside in the Passage Choiseul, while the public paid
fancy prices to see the show. Finally, one evening,
Cupidon had enough of it, and advised the manager
that she would not appear again.*

The good years came to an end with the defeat of France in
the 1870 Franco-Prussian war. The Second Empire fell and so did
the profligate society that gave Cora her reason for being. The end
came after a wealthy young lover, spurned after a torrid affair, shot
himself. He survived to become head of the famous Duval restaurants founded by his father. Cora had to leave Paris. She went
under protest: 'They can't do this to me; I am a public monument'.

Old before her time, in 1884, Cora sold her *Mémoires* to
the publisher Jules Lévy. With the names of her lovers thinly disguised, she spelt out her philosophy:

*I can say that I have never had a favourite lover…A
handsome young and charming man, who has loyally
offered me his arm, his love, his money, has every right
to think that he is really 'my favourite lover', my lover*

for an hour, my escort for a month, my friend for ever.
This is how I understand the matter.

While this never surfaced in her lifetime, a manuscript purporting to be by Cora was published in the early 1980s. This turned out to be a hoax perpetuated by no less than a former chairman of *The Society of Authors*. A restaurant named after Cora is in Henrietta Street.

Another rags to riches story attached to Fanny Murray. Of obscure origins in Bath, the fourteen-year-old Fanny ran away to London in 1743, to find lodgings in Covent Garden. With her 'brown eyes, rosy cheeks and soft features' she soon caught the eye of wealthy rakes who promenaded the Garden. Within three years she was declared to be among the most beautiful women in England. Said one of her admirers, 'It would be a crime not to toast her at every meal'. After an eventful few years enjoying the attentions of the aristocracy, she was rescued from debt by the actor David Ross who proposed marriage. The couple lived together in relative harmony until Fanny's death in 1778.

Crime was endemic to city life. Where money frequently changed hands, as in Covent Garden, there were to be found rogues and vagabonds. In the time of Charles II, paid watchmen, known initially as *Charlies*, spent their nights patrolling the streets or sheltering in huts where they waited the call to action. As the job invariably went to the old and decrepit, their success rate was dismal. Even when caught red-handed, a well-connected culprit could evade punishment by bribing a magistrate. To avoid walking through Covent Garden, those who could afford it took a sedan chair, the taxi-cabs of their day. With two or four chairmen, the occupants were generally safe from molesters. A notorious gang of pickpockets roaming Covent Garden was led by a woman known variously as Jane Webb, Jenny Diver and Jenny Murphy. Her names were legion as were her skills in evading prosecution.

Criminals with style were romanticised as heroes by a gullible public. Many a story, doubtless embroidered, was told of Claude Duval, a young French born highwayman who had a way with the ladies. After his arrest and execution, it was said that the women of London 'of high and low degree' mourned the passing of one who 'even in his heavy French riding boots danced better than the best masters in London'. Awarded a lying in state at a tavern in St Giles, Duval was buried under the central nave of St Paul's. If this sounds unlikely, the parish records mark the burial of a Peter Duval at the date that connects to the highwayman's execution. True or not, his epitaph preserves his image:

Here lies Duval, Reader if male though art,
Look to thy purse, if female, to thy heart.

The Piazza in front of St Paul's was the favoured site for the hustings when the rival candidates for election fought, sometimes literally, for the support of a tightly restricted franchise. Candidates who were rash enough to attempt a general meeting were liable to be pelted with whatever refuse was readily to hand. There were occasions when troops had to be called in to clear the Piazza of rioters.

With jurisdiction over Westminster and Covent Garden, the Magistrate's Court was in Bow Street, so called because it was shaped like a bent bow. Ridiculed for its impotency, the Bow Street court gained stature with the appointment of Colonel Sir Thomas de Veil, a relatively honest practitioner of the law, noted for his harsh sentences, whose weakness was an 'irregular passion for the fair sex'. De Veil's success in breaking up organised gangs did not make him friends in low places. Refusing to compromise, he had to fight off a mob attack on his home and when he died in 1746 his body had to be carried out of the house at three o'clock in the morning to ensure 'a quiet internment'.

De Veil's successor at Bow Street was the dramatist Henry Fielding who was also a qualified lawyer. Having achieved fame as the author of *The History of Tom Jones, a Foundling*, a comic novel that set the standard for English fiction, he was less successful with his stage satires which offended the political elite and led to a clampdown on public performances. Henceforth, it was illegal for any play to be staged without the say-so of the Lord Chamberlain, the keeper of the moral conscience and royal appointee whose role as censor was not ended until 1968.

Fielding's reputation for rakish behaviour started early when he tried to abduct a young lady with whom he was besotted. He again courted scandal when, on the death of his wife in 1744, he married a parlour maid who was already pregnant with the first born of his second family. But a good working knowledge of the law and a growing literary reputation gave Fielding the edge when there came a vacancy for Westminster's chief magistrate.

Taking over the house of Thomas de Veil in Bow Street, Fielding began to dispense justice from this address immediately after his predecessor's death. An honest and forceful defender of justice, he was acutely aware that his job would be made easier by an effective system of crime prevention. As a start in this direction, he managed to secure an annual grant to employ a small force of what he called 'honest thief takers' known as The Patrol.

It was Henry's half-brother, John, his successor at Bow Street, who did most to enforce law and order. Made blind by a botched operation, Sir John Fielding did not allow his afflictions to interfere with his work. Under his leadership the thief takers, now known as the Bow Street Runners, were employed on a more professional basis. With enhanced funding, the Runners came to prominence at a time of increased violence on the highways in and around London. After dark and, on occasion, in broad daylight, anyone who looked as if they might have money in their pockets was liable to be accosted and robbed. A small regular force of Runners kept Fielding busy handing down judgement on a daily flow of nefarious characters.

Under Sir John's direction, the Runners were taken seriously as salaried law enforcers responsible for seeking out villainy in all its guises. Though chiefly accountable for policing Covent Garden, they conducted investigations over a much wider area. Often reported in popular news sheets, their exploits gave a touch of glamour to a risky occupation. The Scotland Yard detective beloved of classic crime fiction has his origin in tales of the Bow Street Runners. The success of the Runners persuaded Parliament that London required a fully trained police force. The Runners had had their day. In 1839, Bow Street, along with other stipendiary magistrates' courts, was restricted to a purely judicial role.

Fielding was often in the news. In 1779, a year before his death, he presided over a murder trial that became the talk to fashionable London. The victim was Martha Ray, an accomplished singer and musician, who had given up a thriving career when she became the mistress of the 4th Earl of Sandwich. Even though the Earl was already married, they lived together openly for sixteen years.

Among Martha's other admirers was James Hackman, half her age, a former army officer whose passion was such that he had given up his commission to become a Norfolk parson, presumably in the expectation that this would give him more of an opportunity to pursue his cause. When it became clear that his attentions were unwelcome, he determined to end both their lives. Armed with two pistols, Hackman waited at the Bedford coffee house for the object of his devotion to appear after attending a theatre. The first shot found its mark but Hickman failed in his attempt at suicide. He was taken to Newgate before appearing at Bow Street where he was sentenced to hang. A desperate request to a fellow clergyman to bring him some poison went unanswered.

A widely circulated broadsheet tribute to Martha contained the indelible lines:

> *A clergyman, O wicked one,*
> *In Covent Garden shot her;*
> *No time to cry upon her God,*
> *It's hop'd He's not forgot her.*

3

Frances Abington, Thomas King, John Palmer, William Smith, by
James Roberts, in Sheridan's *The School for Scandal*, first performed at
Drury Lane on 8 May 1777, courtesy of the Garrick Club, London

Curtain Up

*Punch and Judy; Two new licensed theatres: Covent
Garden and Drury Lane; Nell Gwyn; Theatrical greats
David Garrick, Edmund Kean and Richard Brinsley
Sheridan.*

After the Civil War, the Puritan autocracy led by Oliver Cromwell clamped down on all forms of popular entertainment (Cromwell himself lived in Long Acre from 1639 to 1645 when he moved to Bow Street). But the prudish guardians of public morality could not be everywhere at once. Skilled at avoiding arrest was the *Punch and Judy* man with his simple stage set as easy to assemble as to dismantle if danger threatened. The slapstick mayhem, popular with children and adults alike, caused consternation at St Paul's. The bell to summon the faithful was also adopted as the signal that the *Punch and Judy* show was about to begin. The Church did not welcome the unequal competition as was made clear in a letter published in the *Spectator* on March 16, 1711:

> *Sir: I have been for twenty years Under-Sexton of this Parish of St Paul's Covent-Garden, and have not missed tolling in to Prayers six times in all those years; which Office I have performed to my great Satisfaction, till this Fortnight last past, during which Time I find my Congregation take the Warning of my Bell, Morning and Evening, to go to a Puppet-Show set forth by one Powell under the Piazzas...There now appears among us none but a few ordinary People, who come to Church only to say their Prayers, so that I have no Work worth speaking of but on Sundays. I have placed my Son at the Piazzas, to acquaint the Ladies that the Bell rings for Church, and that it stands on the other side of the Garden; but they only laugh at the Child.*

The appeal fell on deaf ears. With his growing popularity, the puppeteer set up a semi-permanent stage and widened his repertoire. One of his advertisements read:

At Punch's Theatre, in the little Piazza, this present Friday being the 2nd and tomorrow, the 3rd of May, will be presented an opera called the State of Innocence or the Fall of Man. With variety of scenes and machines, particularly the scene of Paradise, in its primitive state, with birds, beasts, and all its ancient inhabitants, the subtlety of the serpent in betraying Adam and Eve etc., with variety of diverting interludes, too many to be inserted here. No person to be admitted in masks or riding-hoods nor any money to be returned after the curtain is up. Boxes 2s; pit 1s. Beginning exactly at second o'clock.

Punch and Judy had its origins in fifteenth century Italy where masked entertainers satirised stock characters from social life. From live actors to wire or string puppets and then to glove puppets was a natural progression to easy-to-produce one man shows. On May 9, 1662 Samuel Pepys noted in his diary that he visited Covent Garden 'thence to see an Italian puppet play... which is very pretty, the best that I ever saw'.

In the early eighteenth century, the leading puppeteer, a regular in Covent Garden, was Martin Powell (he who greatly offended the Under Sexton of St Paul's) who performed with string puppets made of wood. An admirer declared Powell's wires to be 'perfectly invisible, his puppets well-jointed and very apt to follow the motions of his directing hand'.

The stage was itself an elaborate artifice with different scenes rising and falling away while 'flying chariots and fairy cars descended from above'. Punch, with his big belly and little arms and legs, was always the star of the show though he had yet to acquire his hooked nose. Encounters with Joan his 'scolding wife' was already an integral part of the repertoire. Another familiar component was Punch's squeaky voice, created by talking through what was known as a swazzle. With the established popularity of Punch, imaginative efforts were made to broaden his appeal. There was even a puppet production of Shakespeare's *Henry IV* with Punch as Falstaff. But it was as a cartoon character, indifferent to brutality he suffered and inflicted on others, that Punch and his wife, who now became known as Punch and Judy, found an enduring place in the country's folklore.

So ingrained in the public imagination that *Punch* was adopted as the name for the satirical weekly founded in 1841. 'Punch is an English institution', wrote Mark Lemon, the magazine's first editor 'everybody loves Punch'.

The link between Punch and Covent Garden has endured. In his definitive history of Punch and Judy, George Speaight related how in May 1962, some forty 'professors' of Punch and Judy came together to celebrate the tercentenary of Punch's arrival in England:

First of all they gathered in St Paul's church, where the Falstaffian figure of Prebendary Clarence May conducted a special service of praise and thanksgiving for God's gift of laughter as mediated to us through Punch; and then we trooped to Inigo Jones's great portico where a giant Punch booth had been erected. A single Punch appeared first, an antique figure, tall and rather dignified, almost regal; he engaged in some conversation with Clown; rapped the playboard three times; and suddenly a sunburst of Punches sprang into sight – forty of them – squeaking like mad. It was a glorious, an unforgettable sight, that brought tears to the eyes. And the Judies sprang up, kissing and dancing, and a birthday cake was produced with fireworks for candles, out of which cascaded crocodiles, snakes, and dragons. Finally all the Punches grasped a golden cord and, pulling like a tug-of-war team, they unveiled the inscription upon the wall of the church that can be read there now: NEAR THIS SPOT PUNCH'S PUPPET SHOW WAS FIRST PERFORMED IN ENGLAND...1662.

A tradition was established. Henceforth on the second Sunday in May, puppeteers from home and abroad gather to perform in the garden of St Paul's, their day beginning with a procession led by a brass band.

From early days, Covent Garden was a magnet to itinerant showmen who could always be sure of attracting a crowd. So too could the charlatans selling miraculous cures. The self-styled Doctors Rock and Bossy were the leading exponents of sharp practice.

Bossy used to appear in court suit and ruffles and erect
a stage which patients mounted by step ladder. Dr Rock,
on the other hand, came in his carriage, from which
he dispensed his advice and medicine. In his sales talk
Dr Rock maintained that great civic honours had been
offered him by the Lord Mayor but he had refused
them, preferring to give his entire service for the sake of
humanity. At that point of his speech Dr Rock would
produce his pills and offer them to the crowd. He also
advertised in the daily papers and had posters on walls
all over London.

A variety of herbs were in demand for their supposedly curative powers. The trade card of William Blackwell promoted 'all sorts of Physical Herbs, roots, flowers and seeds, green and dried hawthorn, elderberry and juice, leeches and viper, wholesale and retail.' A small cress-like plant known as scurvy-grass was advertised as an antidote to soft gums and a loosening of the teeth. At a tavern on the corner of Henrietta Street, there was lively sale of the scurvy-grass ale which doubtless was as disgusting as it sounds. A broth, made from boiled snails, was said to hold back the ravages of consumption. The essayist, Charles Lamb, noted a drink called Saloop made of Sassafras (a kind of bark) and plants of the cuckoo flower variety, popular as a relief from a hangover. Lamb called it 'the precocious herb woman's darling, much sought after a night out'.

Strollers of sadistic disposition were attracted to the pillory at Bow Street. Those unfortunate enough to be fastened in the stocks were pelted with a ready supply of rotten fruit and vegetables. Nearby was the *Wheel of Fortune* where lottery tickets were sold.

The first theatre in Covent Garden was a converted cockpit. Providing harmless improvised entertainment it was nonetheless the target for killjoys. Demolished by Cromwell's troops in 1659 it was rebuilt as the *Phoenix,* a small, roofed theatre where in its short life, performers found it hard not to offend the authorities.

With the restoration of the monarchy under Charles II, stage performances remained suspect as a breeding ground for disaffection but since the monarch enjoyed the theatre, royal patronage allowed for two new playhouses. One licence went to Thomas Killigrew who had kept company with the King during his exile and who was favoured as an amusing companion. The other licence went to Sir William Davenant a former collaborator of Inigo Jones in the presentation of royal masques. The first to use the proscenium arch and moveable scenery (a wonder of the age), Davenant provided entertainment on a tennis court in Lincoln's Inn.

Killigrew was more ambitious. On a site between Drury Lane, then a narrow dirt track marking the boundary between the City of London and Old Bourn (Holborn) and today's Catherine Street, he built what became known as the Theatre Royal. Opened in 1663, the entire theatre was no larger than the stage of the present Drury Lane Theatre. There were three tiers of seats while at ground level the pit, steeply raked to the rear, had benches covered with green cloth. Lighting was by oil lamps, known as floats, with wicks on pieces of cork floating in a tray of oil. Even so, performances were limited to afternoons and early evenings to take advantage of light.

Drury Lane made Nell Gwyn, the celebrity actress of the Restoration. The story of her life has been heavily embroidered over the years but the popular image of her selling oranges (a fashionable novelty) outside Drury Lane seems to be genuine. Her likely birth place, close to Drury Lane, was in one of the houses cleared away at the beginning of the twentieth century to make way for Kingsway and Aldwych.

Nell made her stage debut in 1665, her sixteenth year, in a play by John Dryden. Opinions vary on her acting talent though she was generally thought to be a witty comedienne. Madame de Sévigné, a French contemporary, praised her as 'young, indiscreet, confident, wild and of an agreeable humour; she sings, she dances, she acts her part with a good grace'. With his sharp eye for leading ladies, Samuel Pepys referred to her as 'pretty, witty Nelly'.

King Charles was no less an admirer. A year after she was first appeared on stage, Nell became one of his several mistresses and probably the only one he truly loved. What a welcome change it must have been for the monarch to enjoy the company of an attractive woman who was neither avaricious nor political. Of her two sons by Charles, the elder by one year was made Duke of St

Albans and, after an army career, served as Lord Lieutenant of Berkshire. The dying wish of her royal lover – 'let not poor Nelly starve' – was met for the two years left to her. She died age 37 or thereabouts in 1687 and was buried next to her mother at St Martin's-in-the-Fields.

After Killigrew's theatre burned down in 1672, Christopher Wren was engaged to design its successor, the foundations of which can still be seen beneath the present stage. Ten years later, shortly before Killigrew's death, the two licensed acting companies merged under the control of Christopher Rich, a thoroughly un-lovable manager who treated actors as chattels. His son, John Rich, made amends by building a new theatre, also confusingly known as the Theatre Royal in Bow Street (henceforth to be known as Covent Garden theatre) where now stands the Royal Opera House. The first production was Congreve's *The Way of the World*.

Popular demand required a larger auditorium but it was a rare actor who had the voice to project across the serried ranks of playgoers. To hold the attention of this audience, managers resorted to spectacular melodramas with so much action as to make the words spoken almost irrelevant. Even so, audiences were easily bored. Wealthier patrons felt free to wander on stage to interrupt the action and show off their latest fashions while the aisles were known as *Fops Alley* for young men parading and flirting. Demonstrations of one sort or another were commonplace.

In December 1762, James Boswell was at Covent Garden for a performance of *Love in a Village*, a comic opera by Isaac Bickerstaffe, when the upper gallery took offence at the presence of two Highland officers. The mob roared out 'No Scots! No Scots! Out with them', hissed and pelted them with apples. Boswell's 'Scotch blood boiled with indignation', he jumped up on a bench roaring, 'Damn you, you rascals' wishing 'from my soul for another battle of Bannockburn'.

Foreign writers never tired of commenting on the bad manners of the English theatre audiences. Karl Moritz, a tourist of the 1780s, was pelted with rotten oranges while 'the occupants of the gallery actually threw glasses of water, injuring the spectators and ruining their clothes'. The gallery held sway over the entertainment:

> There was to be no waiting, even for the King, and if, on arrival, his bow was not deep enough, he would be greeted with shouts of 'Lower! Lower!' On an occasion when one of the young princes did not bow with sufficient respect, the Queen seized his head and forced in down. Once, when the King arrived late, the gallery received him not with the usual clapping, but with unmistakable signs of displeasure. But a London audience was easily appeased. The King took his watch out of his pocket, looked at it and shook his head, as if to signify that he did not know it was so late, whereupon he was rewarded with the accustomed applause, and every one was in the greatest good humour once more.

Acting still carried the stigma of immorality. As late as 1824, Parliament ruled that 'all common Stage Players...shall be deemed

Rogues and Vagabonds' thus keeping company with gypsies, pedlars and beggars. Passions demonstrated on stage were said to encourage unruly or indecent behaviour among the general populace, an argument without much foundation but which carried over to popular novels and, in our own day, what can be watched on screen. Even so, it was with some justification that the theatre was associated with loose living. Syphilis was known as 'Drury Lane ague' while those who spread the disease gave themselves a veneer of legitimacy by claiming theatrical connections. In Victorian times a revealing Q and A joke was popular in male company:

When is an actress not an actress? Nine times out of ten.

One who trod the narrow line between entertainment and degeneracy was Nancy Dawson who, as an early teenager, 'gave convincing proofs of her prodigious and amazing abilities' as a dancer and singer. Such was her popularity that she had her own ballad sung to the tune Here we go round the Mulberry Bush:

Of all the girls in Town
The Black, the Fair, the Red and Brown
That dance and prance it up and down
There's none like NANCY DAWSON.

Yet vainly she each heart alarms
With all Love's hoard of heavenly charms;
She's only for NED SHUTER'S arms
The smiling Nancy Dawson.

But while the comedian Ned Shuter promoted Nancy's career he was certainly not alone in winning her affections which she showered on a succession of wealthy lovers. Her stage speciality was the 'jigg', a dance, often bawdy, performed at the end of a play to send audiences home in a happy mood. Sharing her home was Polly Kennedy, a highly successful courtesan. Their client lists were interchangeable.

It took genius to focus the attention of an audience for the duration of an entire play. For this achievement alone, David Garrick ranks as the first superstar of English theatre. A close friend of Dr Johnson's (they were both born in Lichfield) Garrick's introduction to London was as a wine merchant. In partnership with his brother, Peter, they set up in business in Durham Yard, between Strand and the Thames. But the stage was a powerful magnet for David Garrick, a brilliant mimic who loved to entertain. Garrick's great skill was in conveying reality. Audiences were dazzled by his versatility and by his readiness to make the success of a play by bringing together a team of actors able to match his high standards.

Garrick brought new life to Shakespeare's tragedies. His interpretation of *Richard III* in 1741 propelled him to instant celebrity while his performance as Macbeth had the more sensitive of his audience gasping in horror when he re-appeared after Duncan's murder. Said one critic, 'he looked like a ghastly spectacle, and his complexion grew whiter with every moment' a tricky feat to pull.

In 1747, Garrick raised the capital to buy the lease and the furnishings of the Drury Lane theatre. He remained in command for thirty years before selling out to Richard Brinsley Sheridan who made his name with *School for Scandal*, a work only rivalled in popularity by Oliver Goldsmith's *She Stoops to Conquer,* premiered in 1773. Sheridan was a renowned wit, a talented dramatist and poet, a politician and a charlatan. He spent freely of other people's money and rarely, if ever, paid his debts. One of a succession of duels with an army officer, who had insulted the woman Sheridan intended to marry, was fought outside the Castle Tavern in Henrietta Street. At a subsequent encounter, Sheridan was badly wounded. No-one doubted his courage.

Sheridan's first play, *The Rivals*, was premiered at the Covent Garden theatre in 1775. Two years later his best-known play, *The School for Scandal,* a lampoon of English social pretensions, was produced at Drury Lane. With money in the bank and as sole owner of Drury Lane, Sheridan set about a rebuilding of the theatre. His ambitions outweighed common sense. With seating for over 3,500 in parts of the house actors were inaudible even when shouting at the top of their voices. For the short-sighted not in the front rows it was hard to follow what was happening on stage. It was small comfort to know that a reservoir of water and an iron curtain was the best ever protection against fire. But not good enough.

In February 1809, under-insured and heavily indebted, Drury Lane went up in flames. The blaze was seen across London and crowds gathered to witness the spectacle. Sheridan sat in the window of the Piazza Coffee House with a bottle of wine to comfort him as his dreams evaporated in the heat. When friends commented on his composure, he had a ready response. 'May not a man be allowed to drink a glass of wine at his own fireside?' Master of Drury Lane for thirty tumultuous years, he left the charred remains with a mountain of debt.

Doubts as to whether there would ever be another Drury Lane were stilled when Samuel Whitbread, the wealthy brewer, took on the management of the theatre. Sheridan was forced to resign in favour of a committee of nineteen major stockholders. A new theatre, designed by Benjamin Wyatt, had the same capacity as its predecessor but with improved acoustics and sight lines. A gala occasion with a poetic address by Lord Byron marked the opening in October 1812.

While the interior has had several makeovers and the portico in front and the colonnade at the side were later additions, the theatre today is substantially the same as its reincarnation over two hundred years ago.

In the 1830s Drury Lane and Covent Garden theatres joined forces under the management of Alfred Bunn who economised by engaging artists to work in both houses on the same evening, sometimes with ludicrous results. As Desmond Shawe-Taylor records:

> *Once an impatient Drury Lane audience had to be told that the Scottish tenor, John Templeton, was at that instant completing his performance at Covent Garden with Madame Milbran, and 'if the audience would*

kindly permit the orchestra to repeat the overture, no doubt shortly Mr Templeton would be in attendance.

When Templeton arrived he was bathed in perspiration, and refused to go on as Masaniello until he could get his whiskers and moustache to stick. In the middle of an aria the offending moustache worked its way into his mouth and when the singer flung it away in a fury, it clung 'like an octopus' in the strings of the first violin: an effect which caused the house to rise in a body and cheer.

Another ruse adopted by Bunn was to liven up an evening by interrupting a serious play with high jinks. Marketable actors were not prepared to put up with this. As a leading name in the theatre, William Charles Macready, an actor of uneven temper, took serious objection when Bunn required him to cut two acts from *Richard III* to allow for some light entertainment to be inserted into the programme. Macready wasted no time in discussion. 'Without the slightest note of preparation', reported the aggrieved manager, 'my door was opened and after an ejaculation of "There you villain, take that and that!" I was knocked down, one of my eyes completely closed up, the ankle of my left leg… violently sprained [and] my person plentifully soiled with blood, lamp oil and ink.' In no way apologetic, Macready was taken to court where his victim was awarded £150 damages.

Fire destroyed the Covent Garden theatre, not once, but twice. Tragic though it was, theatrical fires were not exceptional. Notes Desmond Shawe-Taylor: 'What with wooden scenery, muslin transformation drops, guttering candles, back stage draughts, the inadequacy of the extinguishing devices and the irregularity of the fire service, Covent Garden did well, maybe, to have no more than two fires in the two centuries of its theatrical history'.

In his time as Bow Street magistrate, Henry Fielding had strong words for the 'great absence of water...as well as the absence of turn-cocks'. The fire service, such as it was, remained for many years the responsibility of the insurance companies with each maintaining its own engines and turn-cocks.

The tradition of presenting opera at Covent Garden really started after George Frideric Handel settled in London in 1713. His operas written specifically for Covent Garden included *Ariodante* and *Alcina* along with nine oratorios. Not all were successful but Handel's reputation as the country's leading composer was unrivalled in his lifetime.

Opera was again the mainstay of the theatre in the 1840s when it was known as the Royal Italian Opera. Verdi's *Rigoletto* and *Il Travatore* were presented here only two years after their Italian premieres. 'The appearance of the opera prospectus', said the *Illustrated London News* in 1851, 'is anticipated with as much curiosity as a speech from the Throne'.

Between opera seasons there were other entertainments, not all of them worthy of critical acclaim. In 1856, the theatre was let to a Professor Anderson who promised popular attractions including a farce, an opera, a melodrama and a pantomime. According to the dramatist Tom Robertson, the entire season was a disgrace to everyone connected to it.

Soon after the derided professor had vacated the premises another devastating fire broke out. A new theatre designed by Edward Barry, who was also responsible for the Floral Hall, opened in 1858 with a performance of Meyerbeer's *Les Huguenots*. In 1892 the theatre was renamed the Royal Opera House to begin a succession of highlights starting with a production of Wagner's *Ring Cycle* conducted by Gustav Mahler.

The Coronation summer season for 1911, assigned to the Russian Ballet, was judged by one critic to be 'the most significant single artistic event in the first half of the century'. As the presiding genius, Serge Diaghilev introduced British audiences to a chain of masterpieces with Vaslav Nijinsky and Tamara Karsavina in the leading roles. The Russian Ballet became an annual fixture at the Royal Opera House. The Royal Ballet, founded in 1931 by Dame Ninette de Valois, became the resident ballet company at the Royal Opera House in 1946.

One of those actors who leave their mark on theatrical history long after living memories of their performances have faded, Edmund Kean, was an infant prodigy who could recite entire Shakespeare plays. Hyped as *The Celebrated Theatrical Child*, he was hired for bit parts at Drury Lane, not always successfully. In a production of *Macbeth* starring the leading tragedians of their day, John Philip Kemble and his sister Mrs Siddons, Kean played one of the goblins introduced to make the witches seem more spectacular. Doubtless over-eager to make an impact, he pushed too hard against a line-up of child actors causing them to fall over like a pack of cards. The audience loved it though not so Kemble who was made to look foolish, not an experience he relished.

Kean was aged 27 when he made his debut at Drury Lane as Shylock. The omens were not good. A heavy fall of snow two days earlier had left the streets all but impassable as the thaw set in. After only one rehearsal, Kean faced a sparse audience augmented by half-price ticket holders who were less interested in the *Merchant of Venice* than in the farce that was to follow what was supposed to be the main attraction.

Kean did not disappoint. Portraying Shylock as a tragic figure whose every line aroused the sympathy of the audience, he was rewarded with tumultuous applause. The essayist William Hazlitt, drama critic for the *Morning Chronicle*, heralded Kean's appearance as 'the first gleam of genius breaking athwart the gloom of the Stage'.

When, in February 1814, Kean played Richard III at Drury Lane, the theatre was packed to witness his triumph. The *Morning Post* said of it that it was 'one of the finest pieces of acting we have ever beheld, or perhaps that the stage has ever known'. French novelist and historian, Amédée Pichot recorded his experience at Drury Lane when he fought his way into the pit to see Kean. He first inspected the play-bill which was suspended from a leg of mutton in a butcher's shop, and then purchased a sort of bulletin which was sold for two pence by men stationed in Strand, armed with long poles with placards affixed, announcing that they had dramatic journals to sell. This sheet contained the names of the performers and the characters they were to represent, while the second part was occupied with a short criticism of the performance of the previous evening. Later in the day Pichot and his friends took their places outside the pit door. They stood for an hour, jostled by the crowd and threatened by pickpockets, and were finally swept into the theatre in a rush of shrieking women and fighting men, and took their seats.

More praise was heaped on Kean for his Othello and on alternate nights, Iago. Lord Byron and his friends chose not to occupy Byron's private box but to sit in the pit where they were close enough to the stage to see every detail of what *The Times* described as 'a masterly performance'. Samuel Taylor Coleridge spoke for his contemporaries when he said of Kean's acting that it was 'like reading Shakespeare by flashes of lightening'.

But Kean was a flawed genius. His contempt for his audience was notorious. Cast as Charles I in a melodrama he did not like, he got drunk and sent word that 'King Charles had been beheaded on the way to the theatre'. He then took a seat in the auditorium to hurl insults at his understudy.

 Copious drinking did nothing to abate his sexual appetite. Any attractive woman who paid court was fair game. When his affair with wife of a City of London alderman led to a court appearance where damages were awarded to the plaintiff, the press turned against him. In his last appearance in Covent Garden in March 1833, he collapsed on stage. He died, 'a battered relic', a few days later, aged 45.

4

Sir Henry Irving as Matthias in *The Bells*, by F.S.Walker,
courtesy of the Garrick Club, London

From Theatre to Music Hall

*Supper clubs; Music halls; Great days of the Lyceum;
Leading 19th century actors: Charles Mathews, Henry
Irving, Ellen Terry; Oswald Stoll and the Coliseum;
Birth of spectacular theatre; Ivor Novello and Noël
Coward.*

If the drama was barely tolerated by royalty and governments, places serving food and drink were largely free to provide entertainment to attract custom. The lone singer or instrumentalist or even a monologist was seen as no great threat to public order.

Most of these turns are beyond recall and it is not until the mid-eighteenth century that we can begin to detect the origins of the Music Hall in Covent Garden haunts such as the Cyder Cellars and Evans's Supper Rooms where light entertainment could be enjoyed over a round of drinks. Daniel Defoe, in his *Journey through England* describes the Mug-house Club in Long Acre where 'every Wednesday and Saturday...gentlemen, lawyers and tradesmen meet in a great room...a harp plays all the time...and every now and then, one or other of the company entertains the rest with a song'.

Defoe continues:

They have a grave old Gentleman, in his own grey hairs, now within a few months of 90 years old, who is their President, and sits in an arm'd chair some steps higher than the rest of the Company, to keep the whole room in order. A harp plays all the time at the other end of the Room; and every now and then one or other of the company rises and entertains the rest with a song, and (by the by) some are good masters. Here is nothing drank but ale, and every gentleman hath his separate Mug, which he chalks on the Table where he sits, as it is brought in; and every one retires when he pleases, as from a Coffee-house.

21a Maiden Lane was the site of the Cyder Cellars, an all-night tavern attracting a higher class of patron than the Cole Hole, its partner on Strand. Among the regulars were Benjamin Disraeli and Louis Napoleon, an exile in London before a coup brought him back to France to become Emperor Napoleon. William Makepeace Thackeray used the Cyder Cellars as his model for the Back Kitchen in his novel *Pendennis*. Thackeray wrote lovingly of 'jolly singing and suppers at the Cyder Cellars'.

Thackeray's other favourite haunt in Covent Garden was Evan's Supper Rooms at no 43 King Street, now the oldest surviving house looking out on to the Piazza. Completed in 1717, its façade gives its age though the interior, long since ripped out to make space for market produce, has now been adapted for flats and shops. Among the early residents was Sir Kenelm Digby, a versatile, if eccentric, scientist and philosopher whose father had been executed for his part in the *Gunpowder Plot*.

The house was refurbished for the Earl of Orford, better known as Admiral Russell, a royal insider of flexible loyalty whose victories with the Dutch at the battles of Barfleur and La Hogue in 1692, all but destroyed the French fleet. A plaque denotes his residency. No 43 was subsequently converted into what is likely to have been London's first 'family hotel' before it was acquired by W.C. Evans, a chorister at the opera, who opened his supper rooms. His 'singing evenings', with Evans himself loudly applauded for his song *If I Had a Thousand a Year'*, were so successful he built on to the back of the house to allow for a larger audience. Evans stayed well within the bounds of propriety offering 'good English music, as elevating to the mind as it is enjoyable to the senses'. He was described as a 'red-faced, old-fashioned kind of a man' as was Paddy Green his musical director and successor in 1844 as manager.

The diners, exclusively male, sat at long tables listening or half-listening to the entertainers on a large platform flanked by Corinthian pillars. High prices were charged for good food in the tradition of a superior chop house. Fashionable dishes were poached eggs on steak and devilled kidneys seasoned with red pepper. Baked potatoes were served in their jackets. Popular drinks included brown ale, porter, stout and brandy, on tap at all hours of the day and night. Printed in bold on programmes 'Gentlemen are respectfully requested to encourage the vocalists by attention', was an exhortation rarely observed. The highlights of an evening were the comic vocalists headed by Sam Cowell, a UK-born American with a gift for mimicry.

After Evans's closed its doors in 1880, no. 43 was occupied by a succession of short-lived clubs for the literati – the Falstaff, the New, the Pelican and for a short time before it moved to a more long-standing home off Strand, the Savage. From 1891, no. 43 King Street played host to the National Sporting Club, originator of the *Queensbury Rules* and the *Lonsdale Belt*, awarded to the British champion of each weight. Key events were the periodic boxing matches when an audience of up to a thousand members and guests were held enthralled by two muscle men thumping the life out of each other.

An anonymous devotee recalled how:

*We came to its Monday Nights with never-flagging
zest. The comparatively small room - as rooms of
assembly are measured today – had probably held
more men of breeding, of prowess, of brain, of cold-
blooded daring, of dubious present and suspicious past,
of great future, than in any other in the world during
its era of manly entertainment. None of us with an
ounce of imagination, who knew its tough, jocular
environment well, can fail to be stirred when we stand
on its pavement to-day and remember its hectic nights.
It WAS Covent Garden for most of us – for years. A
man's haunt, crude, maybe, but kindly: where no excuse
for failure was proffered or accepted: wherein the fittest
survived and the battle was to be strong. Bless it!*

The National Sporting Club moved to Piccadilly in 1936 and latterly to the Café Royal in Regent Street.

Elsewhere in Covent Garden in mid-late 19th century, once
celebrated entertainers who kept audiences attached to their seats
included Charles Sloman with his talent for 'weaving into a song
any subject proposed by his audience' and W G Ross whose career
was based on an 'infamous' monologue about a murderer facing
his execution. With each verse ending with a bloodcurdling curse
at his audience, 'Damn your eyes', Ross's delivery of *Sam Hall* was
said to 'possess a degree of power amounting to the horrible'.

First performed at the Cyder Cellars in the 1840s, *Sam Hall*
became a kind of rite; if you had never heard it, you had some-

how missed out on a bone chiller that outclassed the excesses of Victorian melodrama. Playing in character, sitting astride a chair in tattered clothes and bedraggled hat, Ross was unforgettable in the role that made his name. It was his only success.

Hugely popular were the *Judge and Jury* shows satirising the judiciary. Presided over by the Lord Chief Baron, Counsel and witnesses were played by professionals while the jury consisted of enthusiastic amateurs. First presented at the Garrick's Head Tavern in Bow Street in 1841, the *Judge and Jury* show moved to the Cyder Cellars where extra seating had to be installed to meet the demand. With the law ever vigilant, increasingly elaborate productions were deemed dangerously close to what we now think of as legitimate drama.

To muddy the waters still further, small improvised theatres transferred well-known plays into entertainments that stayed marginally within the law. So it was that *Macbeth* became a 'ballet of action' with musical backing and rhyming couplets which had Lady Macbeth soliloquising:

> *Is this a dagger I see before me?*
> *My brains are scattered in a whirlwind stormy.*

Staged productions that consisted only of dialogue were still liable to incur heavy fines, not to mention the arrest of performers and even members of the audience. But the popularity of cabaret style arts with professional singers encouraged investment in concert rooms with food and drink served throughout the performance.

From those small beginnings emerged the fully fledged music hall with a succession of variety acts staged in a purpose-built theatre. The range of crowd-pulling acts extended to ventriloquists, illusionists and impressionists. Later came the 'sensations' such as Jules Léotard, 'the daring young man on the flying trapeze' and Charles Blondin, the fabled tightrope walker. Charles Dickens was in the minority who objected to these 'barbaric excrements'.

One of the first music halls worthy of the name was Sans Pareil just off Strand where now stand the Adelphi Terrace and, at the other end of Strand, the Lyceum theatre, originally intended for art exhibitions. Enlarged in 1794 to allow for a small theatre, the Lyceum foundered on the refusal of the Lord Chamberlain to grant a licence. Diverse attractions ranging from the first London exhibition of waxworks of Madame Tussauds to fashionable displays of the mysteries of the East accompanied by 'explanatory readings and other instructive divertissements' kept the place going until 1808 when the Lyceum hosted Charles Mathews with a series of dramatic monologues. Consisting of songs, recitations, character sketches, anecdotes, lectures and improvisations, Mathews was a sensation. The ability of one man to assume a variety of personalities and voices was a remarkable gift and audiences loved him for it.

> *The house was filled, at the first performance, at an early hour. There was only one musician, who played the overture on a piano at the side of stage. The preparations for the entertainment were exceedingly*

simple; they consisted of a drawing-room scene, the
properties being a small table covered with a green
cloth, with a lamp at either side of it and a chair behind
it. Without any other appliance or mean of creating
an effect, Mathews, in evening dress, carried on his
entertainment.

Among Mathews's admirers was Charles Dickens who tried to emulate the master in his public readings by adopting a rapid change of voice and manner to bring to life the characters he had created in his novels. In his biography of Dickens, Peter Ackroyd argues that the portrayals favoured by Mathews – the garrulous female, the urchin, the foreigner with his broken English – 'were precisely the types which Dickens introduces into his fiction'.

Known as the English Opera House from 1816, the Lyceum suffered what the diarist Charles Greville described as a 'magnificent fire' in 1830:

I was playing at whist at the Travellers with Lord
Granville, Lord Auckland, and Ross, when we saw
the whole sky illuminated and a volume of fire rising
in the air. We thought it was Covent Garden, and set
off on the spot. We found the Opera House and several
houses in Catherine Street on fire (sixteen houses), and
though it was three in the morning, the streets were
filled with an immense multitude. Nothing could be
more picturesque than the scene, for the flames made
it as light as day and threw a glare upon the strange

and motley figures moving about. All the gentility of
London was there from Prince Esterhazy's ball and all
the clubs; gentlemen in their fur cloaks, pumps, and
velvet waistcoats mixed with objects like the sans-
culottes in the French Revolution – men and women
half dressed, covered with rags and dirt, some with
nightcaps of handkerchiefs round their heads – then
the soldiers, the firemen, and the engines, and the new
police running and bustling, and clearing the way,
and clattering along, and all with that intense interest
and restless curiosity produced by the event, and which
received fresh stimulus at every renewed burst of flames
as they rose in a shower of sparks like gold dust. Poor
Arnold lost everything and was not insured.

It is always a source of amazement that theatre managers and owners so often failed to insure their property. But with flammable sets and costumes constantly at risk, insurers were liable to charge hefty premiums and impose a parsimonious upper limit on cover. Since every production was a gamble for high stakes it was only a short step to take a chance on the buildings. Theatre investment was not for the faint-hearted.

Responsibilities for the re-build of the Lyceum went to Samuel Beazley, a gifted polymath whose career as an architect allowed time for writing novels and plays. As luck would have it, the re-opening of the theatre, with its grand portico, still with us on Wellington Street, coincided with a relaxation of the law restricting the number of theatres to those granted a royal patent. There was no longer any official objection to the presentation of the classics though theatre managers put their own interpretation on what that meant in practice.

The great days of the Lyceum were from 1871 to 1901 when it was the theatrical home of Henry Irving and Ellen Terry, arguably the most famous partnership in theatrical history. Though today Irving is remembered, if at all, as the archetype of the old style, over-the-top actor for whom subtlety was an alien concept, in his own time he *was* the theatre. As one of his latest biographers maintains, 'It is impossible to assess the Victorian theatre without considering it as a background to Irving'. From humble beginnings in a Somerset village, the young Irving (real name John Henry Brodribb) earned his living as a lawyer's clerk while pursuing his only true interest as an actor able to command the attention of a restless audience. There were no half measures with Irving. Full-blooded melodrama was his natural habitat.

Irving made his name in *The Bells*, a three act melodrama set in Alsace. It was about a respectable burgomaster who is haunted by the memory of a traveller he had murdered for a bag of gold. Fifteen years later, his conscience gets the better of him as he hears the sleigh bells and relives his crime in a delirious dream trial which climaxes with him struggling to pull the hangman's noose from his neck. Said his partner and lover, Ellen Terry, 'Every time he heard the sound of the bells, the throbbing of his heart must have nearly killed him. He used always to turn quite white – there was no trick about it. It was imagination acting physically upon the body'.

Given free rein to demonstrate his talent for conveying diverse emotions with minimum dialogue, Irving entranced audiences who were enthralled, terrified and thrilled in equal measure. Impressionable ladies fainted in their seats.

To say that Irving was single minded is to put it mildly. His treatment of his wife after his triumph in *The Bells* demonstrated his commitment to his art. When, waspishly, Florence asked if he intended 'going on making a fool of yourself like this all your life' it was in a mood of post-natal melancholy that excluded her from the merriment of the first night party. Irving was unforgiving. He stopped the carriage in which they were journeying home, got out and walked away. He neither saw nor spoke to Florence ever again.

Irving's finest moment was also that of the Lyceum, a theatre that was on the edge of financial collapse before *The Bells* filled the house. Free to set his own terms, Irving took over the management of the theatre to launch a run of Shakespearian seasons interspersed with favourite potboilers.

As his leading lady, Ellen Terry projected charm and warmth, personifying the Victorian feminine ideal. But she was a more complicated character than her popular image suggests. An irregular love life producing two illegitimate children had cut across her career. Once partnered with Irving, she knew how to play the game by his rules. While she had as much box office appeal as Irving, she took great care not to bruise his ego. Even when, almost inevitably, they became lovers, the affair was so discreet as to deter the gossip mongers. As Lady Salisbury commented, 'Miss Terry never immoral, only rather illegal'.

Almost as important to Irving as his leading lady was his business manager, Bram Stoker, later to gain fame as the author of *Dracula*. It is not too fanciful to suppose that Stoker found inspiration for his multi-faceted vampire from the chameleon talents of his friend and hero.

Under Irving, the Lyceum became a mecca for popular culture. In his memoir of the 1880s, the journalist J B Booth declared it to be 'something more than a theatre. With the great public...it became a religion to attend the Lyceum, a theatre which ranked as a temple of art, a meeting place for the people and intellectuals of every class and type'.

As the actor-manager in command of all he surveyed, Irving was generous to those of the profession down on their luck. He also entertained on a grand scale. As his biographer Madeleine Bingham records:

At Christmas, when Victorian feelings of warmth and good cheer rose to a climax, Irving's goodwill was shown in practical ways. Every man and woman in the theatre (and there were five or six hundred of them) was presented with a goose, trimmings of sage and onion and apples, and a bottle of gin. The children currently playing were given a goose and a plum cake. In the green-room Christmas Eve was celebrated with punch and a large

Christmas cake. The punch bowl was as vast as Irving's productions, and amongst the ingredients a five gallon keg of old whisky was used to fill it.

On Christmas Eve, 1882 he gave a Christmas Eve dinner to a party of twenty intimate friends...They sat down to spiced beef, roast beef, turkey and plum pudding, and when the flames of the pudding died away and the supper table was cleared, the porcelain was replaced by a roulette wheel and a silk bag containing five pounds' worth of new silver was put in front of each guest.

Lyceum parties to celebrate every success were legendary. The last was in 1902 originally intended to celebrate the coronation of Edward VII. Although the King was ill and the coronation postponed, the curtain went up on Irving's reception.

There were endless rows of tubs of flowers and palms, a Union Jack forming a centrepiece made from thousands of coloured lights, a great crown flaming over a sea of guests, Premiers from all the great colonies, peers and their bejewelled peeresses, statesmen, ecclesiastics, soldiers, artists, men of science, and, most spectacular of all the Indian princes wearing over half a million pounds' worth of jewels – followed closely by men from Scotland Yard.

Everyone was moving and smiling against a backcloth
of crimson velvet, and on the crimson-covered stage, in
the centre of the crowd, stood Irving.

By the turn of the century, the great days were all in the past. The Irving style was under attack by the new drama with George Bernard Shaw leading the charge. The call was for realism on stage, the portrayal of life as it really was but under a critical gaze that pointed out the way to social change.

This was anathema to Irving who sought no more than to entertain. No-one, least of all Irving himself, could imagine this living legend starring in an Ibsen play. It was time for Irving to step aside. He did so reluctantly but in a blaze of glory. He died while on tour playing *The Bells*. The first actor to be knighted, Irving was buried in Westminster Abbey.

Ellen Terry worked on until 1919 when she played the Nurse in *Romeo and Juliet* at the Lyric, Shaftesbury Avenue. Created Dame Ellen in 1925, she was the second actress to be thus elevated. The high point of her late career was the celebration at Drury Lane to mark her fiftieth year on stage. *The Times* called it a 'theatrical debauch'. The report continued: 'From shortly after noon till six o'clock they filled Drury Lane with a riot of enthusiasm, a torrent of emotion, till they were hoarse, laughed to the verge of hysteria'. When she died aged 81 in 1928, it was St Paul's Covent Garden, the Actors' Church that, quite naturally, was chosen as her last resting place. Her memorial tablet is on the South side of the church.

A rebuilt Lyceum opened in 1904. While retaining Beazley's façade, the interior was fitted out in florid Rococo with gold and crimson plush to serve as a music hall. The inter-war period ended on a high note with *Hamlet* played by John Gielgud, the grand-nephew of Ellen Terry. Left empty during the war, the Lyceum was subsequently re-opened as a Mecca dance hall.

A residual claim to fame for the Lyceum came with the 1951 Festival of Britain. As the sales and publicity manager for Mecca, Eric Morley was invited to suggest ideas that might widen the appeal of the Festival beyond its base across Waterloo Bridge on the Thames South Bank. Morley came up with a proposal for an international bathing beauty contest. To enliven the proceedings the contestants would be requested to appear in bikinis, thus displaying more than was customary on such occasions. *Miss World* proved to be hugely popular. After the first title was won by Miss Sweden, the contest became an annual event, hosted by the Lyceum from its inception until 1968. One cannot help but wonder what Henry Irving would have made of it all.

A London County Council plan to build a roundabout on the site to replicate that on the south side of Waterloo Bridge met strenuous opposition from, among others, champions of the Lyceum as one of London's landmark theatres. Its sacrifice for the sake of a traffic island was terrible to contemplate. When good sense and good taste prevailed, the Lyceum was restored to become home to the *Lion King* which started its long run in 1999.

In the dog days of the Lyceum at the turn of the last century, a showman of contrasting style to Irving, was busy on a plan to build London's largest and most splendid theatre. At age 35, Australian-born Oswald Stoll was chairman and managing director of Moss Empires, a music hall circuit that covered the major cities across the country. Stoll's ambition was to create the premier home of variety.

The site chosen for the Coliseum was at the Trafalgar Square end of St Martin's Lane, close to Charing Cross, a busy rail terminus for thousands of suburban commuters who might be persuaded to delay their journey home for an evening of unrivalled entertainment. As the selected architect, Frank Matcham was no stranger to the task having already designed some twenty music halls for Moss Empires. But the Coliseum was by far his most ambitious project to date. It was not simply the proposed size of the new theatre with its 2,939 seats, on a tightly restricted site, that was daunting. Technical challenges included a 160 tonne revolving stage with two concentric rings, Matcham calculated it would need the combined power of thirty electric motors to get it moving. A distinctive feature was a revolving globe at the apex of the tower which was to become a London landmark.

Opening as the London Coliseum Theatre of Varieties, this 'popular palace of entertainment' had a slow start. Variety, as conceived by Stoll, was a cut above the music hall. But his efforts to mark the distinction were not always successful. It was a custom of music halls to announce the next act by a stage hand slipping a number plate into a panel at the side of the proscenium. Stoll aspired to a more dignified introduction. On each side of the stage stood a golden easel, the number of each turn being placed by a regal footman dressed in sumptuous livery of the eighteenth century complete with wig, silk stockings and plush breeches. The audience loved it but not in the way Stoll intended. Loud and prolonged cheers shook the house whenever this splendid figure appeared, his reception far greater than that for the star of the show. The old custom of numbered boards was soon restored.

With variety failing to bring in the numbers Stoll had anticipated, he changed tack in favour of musical comedy. He needed a blockbuster to restore his fortunes. He found it in Berlin where *White Horse Inn*, a Viennese style operetta, was playing to packed houses. The plot, turning on the frustrated love of a head waiter for the glamorous owner of the White Horse Inn, a Tyrolean scenic spot, was incidental to the foot-tapping numbers that had audiences swaying in their seats. It was a huge gamble. London audiences were simply not attuned to operetta beyond Gilbert and Sullivan.

Stoll spent lavishly on the setting for a lakeside inn backed by snow-capped mountains. For the market day scene, the stage was filled with a 150 strong chorus in traditional costumes supported by a menagerie of real life dogs, goats and ponies. The circular stage allowed for a trip around the lake by paddle steamer. Transformed into the approach to an Austrian inn, the Coliseum foyer had girls got up as Tyrolean peasants selling programmes and sheet music.

The Morning Post declared *White Horse Inn* to be 'the success of the century', though James Agate of the *Sunday Times*, doyen of drama critics, damned with faint praise 'the old musical comedy

all over again, only ten times larger'. Stoll could afford to laugh off
the killjoys; he had covered his costs and more with the advance
bookings. *White Horse Inn* ran for 651 performances.

Post World War II, the Coliseum shared with Drury Lane
the great American musicals with *Annie Get your Gun* achieving
the longest run in Coliseum history. Another box office success
was *Guys and Dolls* which opened in 1953. As an illustration
of how critics can get it wrong, Harold Hobson who succeeded
James Agate at the *Sunday Times*, dismissed *Guys and Dolls*, surely
one of the best musicals ever, as 'interminable and overwhelm-
ing and in the end an intolerable bore'. After varying fortunes, the
Coliseum was occupied by the Sadler's Wells Opera Company renamed as English National Opera in 1974.

Drury Lane, meanwhile, experienced wild swings of fortune.
Teetering towards one of the periodic bouts of insolvency in 1935
the theatre found its white knight in the person of composer,
dramatist, actor and producer, Ivor Novello. Like Noël Coward,
with whom he was often confused, Novello came early to show
business having at the age of twenty-one written one of the most
popular songs of the Great War, *Keep the Home Fires Burning*. In
the early 1930s, Coward and Novello were in competition for
West End audiences with Coward packing them in at Drury Lane
and Novello turning out a succession of lightweight plays as star
vehicles, taking the lead role in four of them.

His chance to break into big time musicals came after
Coward's *Cavalcade* closed and Drury Lane was left without a
crowd-puller to fill the vast auditorium. With *White Horse* Inn to

inspire him, Novello had the idea of a Ruritanian style operetta. The synopsis for *Glamorous Night* was written in twenty-four hours and it took less time for the Drury Lane management to decide they were on to a winner. The emphasis was on spectacle – a foundering ship, carriages pulled by real horses, breathtaking scene changes and, above all, melodies that had audiences humming and whistling all the way home. Novello followed with the equally successful *The Dancing Years* with its male chorus which, Novello himself, dubbed 'the prancing queers'. Then came *Crest of the Wave* in 1937, remembered now for its patriotic rouser, *Rose of England*. The most memorable and best of all the Novello melodies *We'll Gather Lilacs* came after the war in *Perchance to Dream* at the Hippodrome.

Novello was a true native of Covent Garden. His flat above Strand Theatre, now renamed the Novello, has a blue plaque recording his residency.

With Noël Coward's *Bitter Sweet* enjoying a long run at Her Majesty's it appeared that the British musical had never been in better health. It was all an illusion. Starting with *Oklahoma,* the first post-war triumph at Drury Lane, the new American, high-energy spectacular musicals engulfed and all but obliterated the British operetta and musical comedy of the time.

Today Covent Garden embraces more than twenty theatres from the Coliseum, Theatre Royal Drury Lane and the Royal Opera House to the Fortune, one of the smallest venues. The first London theatre to be built after the Great War, the Fortune on Russell Street has the distinction of being part over and part under a Scottish Presbyterian church. In the same category of small but cleverly designed theatres, is the Duchess on Catherine Street. Opening in 1929, it found success with plays by J B Priestley and Noël Coward.

5

From *London Town* (1883) showing the
interior of Covent Garden Market

The Ever Changing Scene

The Market thrives; Central Market built; Moss Bros;
Pantomime as annual outing; The arrival of American
musicals; Floral Hall and Jubilee Market.

By the 1830s, Covent Garden Market was thriving as never before. As the Garden expanded so too did the providers of fruit and vegetables bordering the capital. Writing in 1839, historian Thomas Faulkner claimed Hammersmith and Fulham, to be 'the great fruit and kitchen garden north of the Thames for the supply of the London market'. In the early hours, all the roads were crowded with carts on their way to Covent Garden.

In the strawberry season hundreds of women carried the fruit to market in baskets on their heads. Their journey started from Hammersmith and Fulham on the west, Hackney to the north and Deptford and Camberwell to the south. In 1834 the *Saturday Magazine* gave an account of their labours:

A party of these carriers set off with their burdens,
walking at a quick pace and occasionally running so that
they generally accomplish five miles in an hour during
their journey. And it is pleasing to observe with what
skill and address from habit they manage their head
loads, as they are called, seldom having occasion to hold
them with their hands. The burden being placed on

*the top of their heads makes it necessary for the carriers
to keep a very upright posture in walking, so much so
that young persons in the higher ranks of life have been
corrected of a bad habit of stooping by being made to
walk with a small weight on their heads without being
allowed to touch it with their hands, in imitation of
these poor women. The carriers arrive at the principal
fruiterers of London early enough for their customers to
be supplied with fruit gathered the same morning. The
same women meantime proceed with a second load in
London even when the strawberry ground is situated
seven or eight mile from the fruiterers.*

The Gardener's Magazine began reporting on produce and
prices in 1826, the details provided by James Grange who had a
sixty acre garden at Kingsland in North London. His bulletin for
7th February reads:

*Broccoli much injured; the best 2s. per head. Spinage
rather scarce; all common vegetables plenty, but looking
up in price. Asparagus 10s and 12s. per hundred;
inferior 4s. and 5s. Sea cale from 5s.to 7s. per the
measure called a punnet' (an illustration of a punnet
showing a shallow round basket is given), 'apples 16s.
to 20s. per bushel, for the table; 8s. to 10s. for baking.
Pears scarce and dear. Various spring flowers, partially
forced, as crocuses, snowdrops, violets, etc., have made*

their appearance; besides forced bulbs, as hyacinthus
narcissus, Van Thol tulips etc.

With speedier transport on sea and land, produce was bought
in from the Scilly Isles, Holland, Belgium and Portugal. In 1866,
a contributor to the *Cornhill Magazine*, recorded his surprise at
'seeing the market supplied with choice early peas from such an
unexpected quarter as French Algeria'. Exotic fruits appeared,
not all of them from overseas. As early as 1821, Isaac Andrews of
Lambeth celebrated the coronation of George IV with sixty ripe
pineapples grown under glass. Recalling his deprived childhood,
Charles Dickens wrote, 'When I had not money I took a turn in
Covent Garden and stared at the pineapples'.

With the wholesale business increasing alongside retail
shopping, much of the produce arrived in bulk, was sold in bulk
and distributed in bulk. It was not unusual for goods brought to
Covent Garden to be resold in other London markets. The traffic to and fro was a shambles. In his masterly survey of *London
Labour and the London Poor* (1851), Henry Mayhew gives a vivid
impression of all he saw on a typical Saturday in Covent Garden:

As many as 2,000 donkey-barrows, and upwards of 3,000
women with shallows and head-baskets visit this market
during the forenoon. About six o'clock in the morning is
the best time for viewing the wonderful restlessness of the
place, for then not only is the 'Garden' itself all bustle
and activity, but the buyers and sellers stream to and
from it in all directions, filling every street in the vicinity.

From Long Acre to the Strand on the one side, and from Bow-street to Bedford-street on the other, the ground has been seized upon by the market-goers. As you glance down any one of the neighbouring streets, the long rows of carts and donkey-barrows seem interminable in the distance. They are of all kinds, from the greengrocer's taxed cart to the coster's barrow – from the showy excursion-van to the rude square donkey-cart and brick-layer's trusk. In every street they are ranged down the middle and by the kerb-stones. Along each approach to the markets, too, nothing is to be seen, on all sides, but vegetables; the pavement is covered with heaps of them waiting to be carted; the flag-stones are stained green with the leaves trodden under foot; sieves and sacks full of apples and potatoes, and bundles of broccoli and rhubarb, are left unwatched upon almost every door-step; the steps of Covent Garden Theatre are covered with fruit and vegetables; the road is blocked up with mountains of cabbages and turnips; and men and women push past pointing from their crammed aprons, or else their faces are red with the weight of the loaded head-baskets.

...Under the dark Piazza little bright dots of gas-lights are seen burning in the shops; and in the paved square the people pass and cross each other in all directions, hampers clash together, and excepting the carters from the country, every one is on the move...

Inside the market all is bustle and confusion. The people walk along with their eyes fixed on the goods, and frowning with thought. Men in all costumes, from the coster in his corduroy suit to the greengrocer in his blue apron, sweep past. A countryman, in an old straw hat and dusty boots, occasionally draws down the anger of a woman for walking about with his hands in the pockets of his smock-frock, and is asked, 'If this is the way to behave on market-day?' Even the granite pillars cannot stop the crowd, for it separates and rushes past them, like the tide by a bridge pier. At every turn there is a fresh odour to sniff at; either the bitter aromatic perfume of the herbalists' shops breaks upon you, or the scent of oranges, then of apples, and then of onions is caught for an instant as you move along... Then there are the apple-merchants, with their fruit of all colours, from the pale yellow green to the bright crimson, and the baskets ranged in rows on the pavement before the little shops. Round these customers stand examining the stock, then whispering together over their bargain, and counting their money.

Writing two years later, W Moy Thomas, a young writer on *Household Words*, the journal edited by Charles Dickens, found, if anything, the chaos had worsened.

...From all the five inlets to the great square – choked to the throats with every description of thing that goes on wheels – costermongers with baskets, porters in knee-

*breeches, 'hagglers', fruiterers, greengrocers, eating-house
keepers, salesmen and carters swell the restless multitude.*

*They infest the building on all sides; they duck and
bob under upturned shafts; they pour in, denser still,
through narrow passages, and circulate in the maze of
stalls within. Fruit sellers, perched upon boxes, empty out
their cornucopias on the crowd below. Sacks of peas and
potatoes glide down from waggon tails upon the backs of
porters, who grapple their burdens with hooks of steel, and
plunge them into the crowd.*

*I see crews of boarders who dash into waggons and cast
their cargoes overboard; men who clamber to the summits
of towers of cabbages and begin to level them to the shafts;
gangs – whom the crazy Spanish knight would at once
have taken for robbers plundering a caravan – sacking
spring-carts; wholesale buyers who commit tremendous
ravages in the ranks of the flower-pots; Amazons in drab
great-coats with metal buttons, and flattened bonnets,
who lay violent hands upon hampers; brawny giants
bending and straining under deal cases.*

*How they swarm and jostle each other! How they dive
into and cleave a way through the multitude, regardless
of everyman's business but their own!...*

Mythology, on occasion supported by medical opinion,
continued to warn of extraordinary risks attached to eating fruit

and vegetables. With the 1848 outbreak of cholera, the Board of Health cautioned the public against 'every variety of green vegetable, whether cooked or not, cabbage, cucumber and salad... fruit of all kinds, though ripe or even cooked and whether dried or preserved'. Pickles, salted and smoked meat, pork and shellfish were also condemned, as were spirits, lemonade and ginger beer. These old wives' tales did not go uncontested. The Royal College of Physicians published a forthright defence of almost every item of diet depicted by the Board. Abstaining from well-cooked green vegetables might lead to people catching scurvy and thus become more susceptible to cholera. As for abstaining from smoked meat and fish 'nothing promotes the spread of epidemic disease so much as want of nourishment'. Fearing the collapse of his business, a Covent Garden trader had the College of Physicians' opinion reprinted as a placard for prominent display.

The patois of Covent Garden was Cockney or Irish. The Irish basket-women who worked as porters were notorious for their muscle power. One of the Amazonians took a bet that she could carry 'a giant fat man' in a basket from the Market to the Elephant and Castle (some three miles) in twenty-five minutes. 'The *massive load of flesh* being properly placed,' says a contemporary newspaper report, 'the woman started at quick time, followed by a concourse of persons until she arrived at Waterloo Bridge where, according to agreement, she was to have a glass of gin and receive a shilling.' Here the toll-keeper demanded a penny toll for the man in the basket which, after a short and colourful argument, she paid and went on to the toll-gate at the Coburg Theatre where the 'unwieldy gentleman exhibited some uneasiness by thrusting his legs out'. This influenced the betting against her, but by threatening her passenger that she would throw him into the ditch if he did not keep still, she eventually reached the Elephant and Castle within the given time to be greeted by a large crowd, many of whom gave her presents.'

In 1837, a basket-woman carried a tailor from Covent Garden to Brompton for a shilling. The Irish basket-women were celebrated by an anonymous poet:

> *The sturdy form, the very racy brogue*
> *And that mix'd style of dress so much in vogue*
> *With dames you meet beneath the scented shade*
> *Of Covent Garden's flowery colonnade,*
> *Proclaim the honest, humble Irish drudge,*
> *Ready, to farthest suburbs off to trudge,*
> *Crown'd with your purchased flowers – hard-working*
> *Norah!*
> *A somewhat vulgar - but a useful Flora!*

Other colourful characters were described by Moy Thomas:

> *'Look at this grizzly black man with the strawberry*
> *pottles under his arm. Easily he gets along, grinning with*
> *his rows of ivory teeth, because the sellers from their little*
> *fortified citadels call him Uncle Tom. Not a single one*
> *will he lose of those large 'toppers', blushing under the*
> *dark-green leaves.*

Also as this cheerful old man, who has walked all the way from Croydon this morning with a sweet-smelling basket of white flowers which he calls 'double rocket', and all (as he tells me afterwards) for the sake of earning half a crown, less ten pence market fees for his stand under the church.

...Not like that Irish giant, whom I saw just now pitch down and damage a load of cauliflowers, because the owner haggled over the porterage...Thinner and less bustling is the crowd under the Piazza. Hawkers of account-books, dog-collars, whips, chains, curry-combs, pastry, money-bags, braces, tissue paper for the tops of strawberry-pottles, and horse-chestnut leaves for the garnishing of fruit stalls; coffee-stalls; and stalls of pea-soups and pickled eels; basket-makers; women making up nosegays; girls splitting huge bundles of water-cress into innumerable little bunches; and men who write with their toes; possess the Piazza from Great Russell Street to the entrance to the underground saloon of the superior Vocal Entertainment...

Relations between the traders and the Bedford Estate grew ever more fractious with demands for the Duke to justify his substantial income from rents and other charges with structural improvements to make the Market more fit for purpose. The response from the Bedford family was to use its political clout to push through an Act of Parliament confirming their rights granted by royal charter while extending the power of the Estate to control the public thoroughfares and to develop the site as it thought fit. In return, the Duke accepted the responsibility of modernising the Market 'and also of giving to the said Market an Appearance suitable to the present improved and improving State of the Metropolis'.

To replace the sheds and lean-tos with a permanent building, the Estate called on the services of Charles Fowler. While not in the first rank of architects, his track record included the design for a new market at Gravesend in Kent. This consisted of a pair of colonnades connected at one end by a covered building. Fowler proposed something on the same lines for Covent Garden. The model for public display showed a neo-classical Grand Row or Central Avenue, a covered passage with about twenty shops on both sides. Each shop had its own cellar and an upper room for an office or accommodation. The assumption was of fruit and vegetables traders occupying most of the space. Flowers were to be sold at the entrance to the Avenue. Stalls parallel to the Avenue were open to the elements. At the Russell Street end of the Market, the rows were crossed by a colonnade on top of which was a conservatory and terrace with a marble fountain donated by the Duke. It was here that nurserymen displayed their wares. Security was provided by three beadles, conspicuous in their colourful livery, who carried stout truncheons which they were quite capable of using in the event of trouble.

While Fowler's reconstruction of the Market was generally applauded, it did not solve the problem of overcrowding. The wishful expectation that other markets would relieve the pressure proved to be unfounded. The closest rival was the Hungerford Market on the site of what is now Charing Cross rail station. After work started on the railway terminus in 1862, the market had to go. Many of the displaced traders found their way to Covent Garden. The long-standing reputation of Covent Garden as the place to be for attracting business made it nearly impossible to break the tradition.

Frequent disputes with the Bedford Estate led to the setting up of a Market Gardeners and Landed Association. Early demands focussed on providing the stalls on the outside of the Central Avenue with roofing, When this was resisted on the grounds that it would attract 'immoral characters at night', a dubious argument at best since the same argument could apply equally to part of the Market already covered, the stall holders resorted to large umbrellas known as gigs or ginghams. These were tolerated on condition that they were taken down as soon as selling was over for the day, so that the Market cleaners could get to work on clearing the refuse.

More surprisingly a request for public toilets was also turned down. The petitioners had a good case since the existing urinals had been removed as part of the reconstruction, 'causing great inconvenience in there being no place of such kind on the Market for the vast number of persons to resort to'. Ever mindful of economy, the Estate made a sharp rejoinder, reminding the complainants that the old facilities had 'not been done away with till the public urinals adjoining Covent Garden Churchyard had been provided'. At the expense of the Parish, it was noted by the critics.

In the 1860s the Market Gardeners Association was presented with a proposal to create a market on two floors so that everyone could be protected from the weather. There were two objections, the first from traders who used their waggons as stalls for selling their produce. Clearly, they would be faced with a major upheaval if they were compelled to transfer their business to the central market where there was no space for horse drawn vehicles. The second objection was psychological. 'We comprehend that the persons retaining stands in the Lower Market would have a decided advantage over those above it. A revised plan had the ground floor reserved for cheaper, bulk produce such as potatoes and carrots leaving the upper floor for fruit, vegetables and flowers. However, the consensus remained in favour of a level market.

Radical change could not be put off indefinitely. With the Market growing busier by the month, it was a constant complaint of those who lived in Covent Garden that all the streets leading into the Market were clogged with traffic. Street widening provided some alleviation. Wellington Street built to connect Waterloo Bridge with Bow Street was a great improvement on the constricted Charles Street which it supplanted. Slum-riddled alleys were demolished to make way for an upgraded Tavistock Street while Exeter Street was opened onto Strand. In 1855, Long Acre was extended into the newly built Garrick Street. While the Bedford Estate made a substantial contribution to these improvements, thus augmenting its investment in Covent Garden, the bulk of the cost was born by the Metropolitan Board of Works, responsible for London's infrastructure.

Among the beneficiaries were the businesses loosely attached to the Garden but attracted to a thriving neighbourhood. Long Acre, for example, was the home of coach builders. It is a safe economic prediction that a successful enterprise will attract others of like occupation. In Long Acre the trend was set by John Saunders who sold his first coaches in 1695. By the end of the eighteenth century, Long Acre boasted twenty-five coach builders along with as many saddlers and other related crafts.

An 1880 guide for French visitors to London devoted a section to buying a coach, presumably for an onward journey. The suggested questions and the likely responses from a persistent salesman were given in French and English.

> *Salesman: 'I think it will suit you: it is well hung (suspended) and goes very easy.'*

> *Customer: 'But is it strong?'*

> *Salesman: 'Strong? Why just look at those steel springs, those shafts, and those iron axles with their brass boxes (with their patent boxes). They are made to last for ever.'*

> *Customer: 'The wheels seem to me very light.'*

> *Salesman: With those wheels you might make the tour of Europe. I will warrant them a year.'*

> *Customer: 'The body appears to me very low.'*

Salesman: 'Travelling carriages should not be too high,
they are then so easily overturned.'

Customer: 'Open the door and let down the steps.'

Salesman: 'Examine the inside well. Observe this fine
cloth and handsome lace, these spring cushions, equally
soft and convenient, these pockets, the net for hats,
the blinds and the curtains. You see there is nothing
wanting.'

All of which goes to show that sales patter has remained consistent through the ages. Indeed the same questions and answers would have been heard when the coach builders were succeeded in Long Acre by car showrooms.

In King Street was an auction house that specialised in second-hand clothes. A frequent attender in the 1840s was distinguished by a black skull cap and a blustery beard. This was Moses Moses, later known as M Moss, who had been born into the Jewish community of London's East End. Like so many immigrant families, Moses started young in the rag trade building up a business that did so the well he was able to lease two shops in King Street. This was the start of what became Moss Bros, the world famous place to go for hiring smart wear for big social occasions.

Moses was succeeded by his two sons, Alfred and George, who officially adopted the name of Moss Bros in 1898. With Alfred as the salesman and George, who was profoundly deaf, as the tailor, the business expanded into selling new, readymade clothes for the upper end of the market.

The next development came after a music hall comic paid for the loan of a set of tails for one of his monologues. When his example was followed by other customers who were happy to pay a hiring charge rather than fork out for clothes that were rarely taken out of the wardrobe, a Hire Department was set up to satisfy their needs. Expanding into premises on the corner where Garrick Street meets Bedford Street (now a Tesco Express), the stock of clothes to hire grew to include society weddings, Ascot, fur coats and hats for a visit to cold climates, lightweight outfits for tropical cruises and even robes traditionally worn by peers of the realm for royal occasions.

Moss Bros continued to thrive under Harry Moss who started on the lower rungs at age 13 and took over as managing director in 1921 when he was just 25. An enthusiast for direct marketing, Harry built up the Moss Bros reputation for sartorial quality for hire or sale at reasonable prices.

Though indelibly linked to Covent Garden, Moss Bros now known simply as Moss, has long since departed its flagship shop though it returned briefly to its original premises in King Street. Sold to private equity in 2020, the name of Moss is familiar to customers at 125 stores countrywide, though, sadly, not in Covent Garden.

Another revered business name linked to Covent Garden is Stanfords, the first stop for tourists and travellers in search of maps, guides and books about adventures in distant parts. The shop, originally in Charing Cross Road before moving to larger premises in Long Acre, was founded by Edward Stanford, for many years the only map maker in London. A major achievement was the *Library Map of Europe*, the work of cartographer John Bolton, published in 1858. A family business to 1947 when it was sold to George Philip and Son, Stanfords can now be found in Mercer Walk.

To change gear from the sublime to the ridiculous, Covent Garden was for many years the home of pantomime with the Theatre Royal, Drury Lane and the Lyceum leading the Christmas festivities. Visitors to Britain might well have wondered what all the fuss was about. How did folk tales and nursery stories get mixed up with music hall turns, actresses in thigh boots posing as men and comedians in petticoats? The origins of pantomime (literally a mime show though it was never really that) go back to the 1720s when dances by harlequins were part of any production whether tragedy or comedy. Over time, these entertainments were relegated to 'after-pieces' to round off an evening in the theatre with Harlequin, the resourceful hero, Columbine the heroine, Pantaloon, the old fool and the Good Fairy. David Garrick had no patience with this. Despising pantomime as a distraction from legitimate drama, under his management of Drury Lane the panto was limited to the Christmas season. So began a three hundred year old tradition that still delights children of all ages.

The theatre historian, W. Macqueen-Pope had his own memories of Drury Lane and the Lyceum when, in the early part of the last century, pantomime was king. Eating and drinking were as much fun as what went on the stage.

An observer, getting down to those two big playhouses about 10 a.m. would have found them surrounded by large queues waiting for admission to the cheaper and unreserved parts. There would be kind mothers and fathers, uncles and aunts taking the dear children to the pantomime. All the grown-ups – the female grown-ups – would be clutching baskets, string bags or receptacles of some kind – and in them all was food. Although it would be hours before the doors opened, every pair of jaws in those queues would be steadily munching, whilst vendors of sweets, peanuts, popcorn and what you will, did a steady, roaring trade. When the doors opened there was a rush and scurry for places. As soon as they were seated, out came those baskets and bags and steady eating was indulged until the curtain rose – pies, sandwiches, cakes, hard-boiled eggs – portable "solids" of every kind. All through the first half of the show, sweets were sucked or chewed. Then, in the interval – tea. This was ordered from attendants and reinforced by whatever was left in the bags. Second half meant sweet consumption – non-stop- once again. At Drury Lane there were always twenty-five extra cleaners at pantomime time to clear away the debris between the shows.

At *Babes in the Wood*, the last pantomime at Drury Lane before the Second World War, Macqueen-Pope witnessed:

At the third matinée, a party of six in the second row of
the stalls, who as soon as the curtain was up, produced a
luncheon basket. From it they took knives, forks, plates,
spoons, cold chicken and salad, sweets and a little cheese.
They had an excellent lunch and thoroughly enjoyed
it. It was, of course, possible to look at the stage between
courses.

Over at the Lyceum, a reviewer on the journal *Theatre World*
urged a visit to the pantomime just 'for a glimpse of the most
wonderful audience in London':

While the children are home from school you will find
this huge theatre – the seating capacity is over 3,000 –
packed to the doors with an enthusiastic crowd, most of
whom are children, who are not bored with every type
of theatrical entertainment, but who have come to enjoy
themselves. And they do – thoroughly. The screams of
laughter and deafening applause which greet every song
and every scene is the most cheerful sound in the West
End.

At the corner of Catherine Street is a water fountain com-
memorating Augustus Harris who, at the age of 28, became the
youngest manager in the history of Drury Lane. Harris believed
in spectacle to bring in the crowds. Under his reign, pantomime
entered the age of extravagance, with elaborate sets and top casts,
mostly from the music hall, revitalising familiar routines in lavish

costumes that needed a small army of dressers to give verisimilitude to fantasy.

Harris was still in his thirties when he took on the joint management of Drury Lane and the Royal Opera House. His talent for mounting large scale productions served him well at the Opera House where he gave the best singers from across Europe the chance to perform on magnificent stage sets. In 1891 Harris was knighted though, ironically, not for his services to the theatre but for happening to be Sheriff of the City of London during the state visit of Kaiser Wilhelm II. 'Clever, ambitious, bubbling over with infectious energy', Harris worked himself to death at the age of forty-four.

A turning point for Drury Lane came in the inter-war years when American musicals were imported into the West End. The 1925 success of *Rose Marie* at Drury Lane persuaded the management to let it run over Christmas, prompting *Theatre Record* to note that 'pantomime seems nearly dead in the West End nowadays'. But in provincial theatres across the country, the tradition lived on and remains today as popular as ever.

Now part of the Royal Opera House, the magnificent Floral Hall, an L-shaped construction almost entirely of glass and iron with a dome fifty feet across, was designed by Edward Barry. It is often assumed that the Floral Hall was a homage to Joseph Paxton's Crystal Palace built in Hyde Park for the 1851 Great Exhibition. In fact, a number of glass buildings pre-dated the Crystal Palace and the Floral Hall, including those at Syon House in Brentford, Hungerford Market in London and a conical glass house at Bretton Hall, near Wakefield. As chief gardener to the Duke of Devonshire, a keen horticulturalist, Joseph Paxton had long been testing out his ideas for a greenhouse, all of glass and iron, for the cultivation of all manner of fruit and vegetables.

In London, on what is now the site of Hackney Town Hall, the German born Joachim Conrad Loddiges created rain forest conditions in the world's largest hothouse to produce, said the Botanical Magazine, 'many rose exotics into our gardens'. The Loddiges tropical palm house pre-dated Decimus Burton's palm houses at Kew by 24 years.

Covent Garden's Floral Hall, inaugurated in 1860 with a grand ball attended by the highest in high society, led by members of the Royal Family, was used for promenade concerts for a year before it was handed over to the Market florists. *The Times* reported on 'a splendid collection of flowers of every kind, all of which are marked for sale in plain figures...tables are laid out as at a large dinner, open spaces being made at regular distances so that visitors may walk about without interruption. In the centre is a large circular raised slab filled with flowers of every imaginable description'. There was even carpeting in the gangways.

The Floral Hall continued to host balls and other social events, mostly in the winter months when fresh flowers were rare. This changed when imports and improved horticulture allowed for the more affluent homes to be decked with flowers throughout the year. Concerts were summarily banished after a Saturday evening in 1865 when an audience was turned away at the last minute by a notice from the Duke of Bedford, via a solicitor's letter, declaring 'the immediate suppression of music', an order, that at first reading, seemed to imply a general ban but in reality applied only to the Floral Hall. Such was the tact and sensitivity of the legal and landed establishment.

On the other hand, while the Floral Hall was closed to music and dancing, the Royal Opera House more than compensated, not just with its stage productions but by devoting its vast space from October to April to masked balls. These were not cheap affairs as Macqueen-Pope recalled:

> *Your ticket cost a guinea, which allowed you to dance. If you simply wanted to be a spectator, you could go into one of the great circles at the Opera House and look for a few shillings. But that was not much good. You had to participate in the fun if you wanted the full flavour. You were expected to be in fancy dress and masked. You could, however, hire a domino and a mask on the premises to cover your evening dress, and that saved a lot of trouble.*

> *All the 'ladies' wore masks during the early part of the ball, which did not start until midnight, although they shed them later. Sometimes, however, a couple would arrive and both wear masks all the time. You drew your own conclusions from this, and perhaps you might, without knowing it, one day read the sequel in a report of a sensational divorce case in the evening papers.*

There was always plenty to eat and drink served from long bars with attendants dressed in red, white and blue. Champagne was the drink of the night. 'After the ball was over', as the popular song had it, 'after the break of day', revellers made their unsteady way to one of Covent Garden's 'all-night' pubs for early breakfast of eggs, bacon and coffee.

Inevitably the Covent Garden ball found its way into the life of Bertie Wooster, the archetypal silly ass, created by P.G. Wodehouse. Here is Bertie reflecting on the strain of having to cope with two irrepressible young cousins:

I suppose the fact of the matter is, I'm not the man I was. I mean those all-night vigils don't seem to fascinate me as they used to a few years ago. I can remember the time, when I was up at Oxford, when a Covent Garden ball till six in the morning, with breakfast at Hammams and probably a free fight with a few selected costermongers to follow, seemed to me what the doctor ordered. But nowadays two o'clock is about my limit; and by two o'clock the twins were just settling down and beginning to go nicely.

If half of what was said about Covent Garden balls is true, we can sympathise readily.

Even with the Floral Hall handed over exclusively to flowers and fruit auctions, market space remained at a premium. In August 1870, the *Gardener's Chronicle* went on the attack:

The London Flower Market has long been a disgrace to the metropolis. Inadequate in size, ill-suited for its purpose, in bad repair, a dilapidated shed, in fact, it has long been an eye-sore and a laughing-stock to bystanders and a source of vexation and annoyance to those whom business leads into its precincts...

After a decade when little had changed, the traders found themselves an influential ally. In August 1880, the first in a series of articles demanding a radical overhaul of Covent Garden in the public interest, appeared in *Punch*, a satirical weekly, mild by current standards, but with a middle-class readership that constituted a powerful lobby. With offices in Bouverie Street, a short step from King Street, the writers at *Punch* had first-hand knowledge of the Covent Garden shambles. Renaming it Mud Salad Market, *Punch* attacked what was seen as an obsequious Board of Guardians for allowing the Bedford Estate to occupy public highways to create 'the greatest nuisance ever permitted in a great city of nuisances'. The Market declared *Punch* 'glories and thrives in its filth'.

Who was to blame? The Duke came in for a drubbing for doing little in return for the rents he collected from shop-keepers and stall holders, not to mention the tolls imposed on all produce entering the Market. But the culpability was shared with the

Metropolitan Board of Works (MBW) whose directors balked at funding road improvements that, arguably, were the responsibility of the Bedford Estate. It must be added that while the MBW had many achievements to its credit, not least a modern sewage system and the inauguration of a numerous parks and open spaces, the way it did business, handing out contracts to builders who were not averse to offering financial incentives to gain precedence in the pecking order, damaged the reputation of what was commonly known as the Metropolitan Board of Perks. While there is no direct evidence, it is likely that the Bedford Estate declined to play the game of passing the brown envelope.

Expectations were raised when in, 1889, the MBW was succeeded by the directly-elected London County Council. However, it was the Bedford Estate that took the initiative in clearing the houses on Tavistock Row to create a site for the purpose-built market, to be known as the Jubilee Market, for the sale of vegetables on the ground floor and imported flowers on the first floor. Meanwhile, the New English Fruit Market under a glass roof began to take shape on the site of the old Bedford Hotel in Russell Street.

Elsewhere in Covent Garden, independent of the MBW and the Bedford Estate, a more ambitious building programme was underway. It started when an American philanthropist, George Peabody, whose ancestors came from Hertfordshire, set up a trust to build what we would now call social housing in deprived areas of London. Covent Garden with it army of casual labour, was a prime candidate for relief. On land cleared on Wild Street, off

Drury Lane, work started on 13 seven-storey blocks of flats. As they began to take shape the public reaction was of startled disbelief. High buildings with multi-level accommodation, though increasingly common across the Channel, were virtually unknown in London.

Peabody flats were in no way luxurious. The rooms were small and so too were the windows. With austere outward appearance, the buildings gave the impression of a barracks, designed for Spartan living. There was just one communal lavatory on each floor with a washroom at ground level. None of this was any deterrent to the many working-class families accustomed to much inferior conditions. Prospective tenants were carefully vetted. A reputation of good repute was the first condition of tenancy.

The Peabody Estate, minus two blocks that were demolished after suffering war damage, the rest thoroughly modernised, is still with us, a tribute to a remarkable visionary who helped set the tone for social reform.

6

Dickens, aged twelve, at the Blacking Warehouse

The Covent Garden
of Charles Dickens

*Dickens's weekly journals: Household Words and All
Year Round; Novel serialisations; The Six Toes Trial;
Boom in book and periodical publishing; The Strand
Magazine.*

Let us be clear, the much visited Old Curiosity Shop on Ports-
mouth Street at the south corner of Lincoln Inn Fields, is not the
Old Curiosity Shop of the Dickens novel. The full story is told in
an excellent article by Lee Jackson to be found on the Charles
Dickens Museum website. As it is only marginal to our story, it
is sufficient here to say that the myth has its origins in the 1880s
when an enterprising retailer enhanced the appeal of this ancient
building by inscribing the masonry with the legend 'The Old Curiosity Shop, Immortalised by Charles Dickens'. Thousands of
tourists, chiefly from America, took him at his word while boost-
ing the shop's appeal with the widespread reproduction of photo-
graphs and paintings.

All that said, Covent Garden and Strand abound with undis-
puted links to Charles Dickens. The first place of work for one of
England's greatest novelists was in the squalid neighbourhood just
off Strand bordering the River Thames. Charles Dickens was just
twelve years of age when he was taken on by Warren's Blacking of
30 Hungerford Stairs, a manufacturer of boot blacking. A fellow

worker, a boy called Bob Fagin, told Dickens what to do. Small earthenware containers of boot blacking had to be prepared for sale. Dickens's job was 'to cover the pots of paste-blacking with a piece of oil-paper, and then tie them with a string; and then to clip the paper close and neat all round.' When he had finished a few gross of these, 'I was to paste on each a printed label'.

He worked for ten hours a day with a break at twelve for a bite to eat and again in the late afternoon. The sheer tedium of the job made for nightmares as too did the dismal premises of his employer:

A crazy tumbledown old house, abutting of course on the river, and literally overrun with rats. Its wainscoted rooms and its rotten floors and staircase, and the old grey rat swarming down in the cellars, and the sound of their squeaking and scuffling coming up the stairs at all times, and the dirt and decay of the place, rise up visibly before me, as if I were there again.

Memories, however torrid, fed his imagination. He drew on his experience for the moulding of the house with a Thames wharf behind it in *Nicholas Nickleby's* 'dark and broken stairs' where Fagin lives in *Oliver Twist* and for the Thames summer-house of *The Old Curiosity Shop*, 'in a crazy building, sapped and undermined by the rats, and only upheld by the great beams of wood which were reared against its walls'.

Today, a blue plaque at the corner of Chandos Place and Bedford Street commemorates Dickens's early days. A second plaque is on the corner where Tavistock Street meets Wellington Street. It was here that Dickens had his editorial offices for his weekly journal *All the Year Round*. By then Dickens was forty-seven and at the peak of his literary eminence. Covent Garden Market held a particular fascination for him. As he wrote in 1836:

> *Covent-garden market, and the avenues leading*
> *to it, are thronged with carts of all sorts, sizes and*
> *descriptions, from the heavy lumbering waggon, with*
> *its four brave horses, to the jingling costermonger's cart,*
> *with its wheezing donkey. The pavement is already*
> *strewed with decayed vegetable-leaves, broken hay-*
> *bands, and all the indescribable litter of a vegetable*
> *market; men are shouting, carts backing, horses*
> *neighing, boys fighting, basket-women talking, piemen*
> *announcing the excellence of their pastry, and donkeys*
> *braying. These and a hundred other sounds form a*
> *compound discordant enough to a Londoner's ears, and*
> *remarkably disagreeable to those of country gentlemen*
> *who were sleeping at the Hummums for the first time.*

Hummums was the former Turkish bath house lately converted into a hotel.

All the Year Round was Dickens's second venture into the periodical market. The first, *Household Words* had failed to satisfy his desire to have complete editorial control. Though intending to give wide coverage of social issues, the success of *All Year Round* was dependent on novel serialisation, the first of which was Dickens's very own *A Tale of Two Cities*. This was succeeded by *The Woman in White* by his friend Wilkie Collins.

The Woman in White began serialisation in November 1859. As it followed immediately on the last episode of *A Tale of Two Cities*, much was riding on Wilkie's most ambitious project to date. Dickens had no cause to worry. The story of a conspiracy to defraud the wealthy and beautiful Laura Fairlie, by having her confined to an asylum, excited readers already acquainted with scandals associated with the false diagnosis of mental illness. As the circulation of *All the Year Round* climbed above 100,000, queues of anxious subscribers gathered outside the journal's offices whenever a new instalment was expected. *Woman in White* bonnets and perfumes went on sale. There was even a fashion for *Woman in White* quadrilles and waltzes.

Wilkie's other great success, *The Moonstone,* which set the trend for thousands of mystery novels, ran for thirty-two episodes over eight months in *All the Year Round* during 1868. Dickens came to dislike the book. 'The construction', he said, 'was wearisome beyond endurance'. But, it is a fair guess that *The Moonstone* was the inspiration for his *The Mystery of Edwin Drood*.

Dickens had an eye for talent. Several journalists who were recruited to *Household Words* and *All the Year Round*, went on to great glory. Leading the band of larger-than-life characters was George Augustus Sala. After joining *Household Words*, he wrote a series of articles on London life called *The Key of the Street*. When the collected edition came out, Thackeray, who was not given to excessive praise declared it to be 'one of the best things I have ever read'. Sala followed up with *Twice Round the Clock*, an hour-by-hour account of the city at work and play, published in the weekly journal, *The Welcome Guest*. The journalist J.B. Booth described Sala 'resplendent in glossy top-hat, wonderful frock coat and immaculately starched white waistcoat', a stout figure made instantly recognisable by his 'gargoylesque nose'.

The high point of Sala's career was as a feature and leader writer for the *Daily Telegraph*, where he delighted his readers with a florid style that passed for sophistication. Coffee was 'the fragrant berry of Mocha'; blood, 'the crimson stream of life'; a dog's tail, his 'caudal appendage'; while the humble oyster was 'the succulent bivalve'. His *Dictionary of National Biography* entry catches the essence of the man.

The facility with which Sala drew upon his varied stores of half-digested knowledge, the self-confidence with which he approached every manner of topic, the egotism and the bombastic circumlocutions which rapid productions encouraged in him, hit the taste of a large section of the public.

Money problems were endemic to Sala who was made bankrupt in 1895. Living hand to mouth did not deter the mercurial Sala from resorting to the law to compensate for real, or more often, imagined slights. One of his gossip-worthy disputes was with the *Punch* artist and caricaturist, Harry Furniss. It began with a Furniss lecture on portraiture. A stinging attack in the *Telegraph*, unsigned but unarguably Sala's work, accused Furniss of a half-hearted presentation. To add to the artist's sense of grievance, the paper refused to publish his response. He then picked up on an amusing but unsubstantiated story that Sala had failed his admission to the Royal Academy of Art School because his drawing of the human foot had six toes. When Furniss repeated the tale in another of his lectures, claiming that as a result of Sala's rejection by the RA he had become the *Telegraph's* art critic, the *Westminster Gazette* followed with a cartoon showing a six-toed Sala threatening a diminutive Furniss.

Sala demanded an apology which Furniss, who was not in any way responsible for the cartoon, refused to give. The nonsense was perpetuated by a court action when the substantial damages to Sala suggested by the judicial summing up, evaporated with the jury's token award. The Great Six Toes Trial became the joke of the month in the music hall where it was known as a case of 'out of the Furniss into the fire'.

The phenomenon that was Charles Dickens both thrived on and helped to accelerate a publishing boom, initiated by the removal of taxes on knowledge and new technology. Writers were carried along on a rising demand for entertaining and instructive literature. William Cobbett's *Weekly Political Register* opened the way to a cheap radical press. Taxes on press advertising went in 1853 and on newspapers two years later. Duties on paper were lifted in 1861.

Steam power revolutionised printing. The four-cylinder press adopted by *The Times* was in use by 1828; the rotary press by 1857. Cheap wood-pulp paper and new paper-making machines brought down production costs for books and journals. Having dropped its price to a penny, the *Daily Telegraph's* circulation increased to 300,000. The *Illustrated London News* launched in 1842, opening the market to picture journals.

Libraries came on stream, many associated with Sunday schools, literary and philosophical societies, even public houses. The Public Libraries Act of 1850 opened the way to financing libraries on the local rates. New writers were sponsored by Charles Mudie with his 'circulating' library. Favouring the three-decker novel as a means of holding customer loyalty (subscribers could only borrow one volume at a time), Mudie was so successful, publishers adapted their output to suit his needs. In return for a high discount, Mudie was prepared to support a novel, tailored to middle class taste, with advance orders of several hundred copies.

With the 'railway mania' adding three thousand miles of tracks between 1843 and 1848, allowing for fast and economical distribution, new fiction was on a steeply rising curve. Dickens did much to satisfy the demand and not simply by writing. He loved acting and actors. At age 20, he angled successfully for an audition at Drury Lane but a heavy head cold caused him to pull out at the last moment. Thereafter, with writing taking up more of his time and with the success of *Sketches by Boz* and *The Pickwick Papers*, he gave up on the stage as a full-time career while participating enthusiastically in amateur productions to raise money for charitable causes.

While Dickens's thespian talents were judged to be modest, it was a different story when he took to the stage as a reader of his own work. Modelling himself on Charles Mathews, famous for his *At Home* impersonations at Drury Lane, Dickens perfected the skill of changing his voice to represent stock characters – the garrulous woman, the quick witted urchin, the foreigner with broken English – he had encountered on his wanderings in Covent Garden and surrounding districts.

The cultural milieu of Covent Garden was a big attraction for book and periodical publishers. At its peak, Covent Garden accounted for twenty-seven publishing houses. In the early twentieth century, Henrietta Street was the editorial address for Macmillan, Duckworth, Pearson, Heinemann and Chapman & Hall. The illustrious author list for the last all included Dickens, Thackeray, Mrs Gaskell and Robert Browning.

The radical publisher, Victor Gollancz, held sway at 14 Henrietta Street. He founded the *Left Bookclub* where authors tore into the Conservative Party for its economic and social shortcomings. In the depressed years of the 1930s, Gollancz was a tireless promoter of humanitarian causes, not least campaigning for aid to Germany after the defeat of Nazism led to mass hunger. In austerity Britain held down by rationing of even basic foods, he faced an uphill task. His critics pointed out that Gollancz himself did not set a good example. On most days he could be found at the Savoy enjoying an expensive leisurely lunch. 14 Henrietta Street is now a boutique hotel.

Running into Strand from Covent Garden is the tiny Burleigh Street named after Sir William Cecil (Lord Burleigh), Queen Elizabeth I's Chancellor whose mansion occupied the space. It was here in January 1891 that the first monthly edition of *The Strand Magazine*, the brainchild of printer and publisher George Newnes, went on sale. *The Strand* was a general interest periodical with fiction as its backbone. Sherlock Holmes made his first appearance in *The Strand* as did the inept Bertie Wooster and the inimitable Jeeves. Other notable contributors who graced the pages include Rudyard Kipling, Agatha Christie and W. Somerset Maugham. An outstanding feature of the magazine was its striking front over with its view of Strand from the corner of Southampton Street. The drama critic, Alan Dent who lived in Covent Garden and wrote about it tells of the powerful impact the famous cover made on him as a child visitor to London.

> *In the middle distance... a newsboy ran across the*
> *street, another stood on the kerb nearest to us. On*
> *the pavement on the left a young lady with a folded*
> *umbrella walked towards us, and an old gentleman*
> *with a furred collar to his coat walked away from us. A*
> *gent approached in a tall hat, and a bobby stood on the*
> *edge of the pavement. Two hansom cabs approached,*
> *one on either side of the street. This jacket was to the*
> *eyes of my infancy the quintessence of the London of my*
> *longing; and the same view is to me the quintessence of*
> *London still. Almost always this cover was a pale duck-*
> *egg shade of green, but when it came to December (or*
> *Christmas) number it was night-time and thick snow*
> *was falling – on the same personages in the same scene*

– a magical transformation into winter, like that in the
Christmas pantomime.

After its circulation settled at around half a million, the *Strand Magazine* moved a few yards west to Southampton Street where it joined an associated group of family journals that appeared under the Newnes banner. Squeezed between rising costs and falling circulation, *The Strand* closed in 1950. Its influence, however, endured for many years with the bound copies kept in public reference libraries.

7

The exterior of the Garrick Club, by Frank Marrable,
courtesy of the Garrick Club, London

All the World's a Stage

*The founding of the Garrick Club; Characters of the
Club; Unrivalled collection of theatrical paintings; The
Milne legacy; Free speech and the Muggeridge affair.*

One of the prominent buildings in Covent Garden is the Garrick Club, appropriately on Garrick Street. (Full disclosure, I have been a member for many years). The Club had its start in 1831 when a coterie of drama enthusiasts wanted a place where 'actors and men of education and refinement might meet on equal terms', a radical enough proposal at a time when those who made their living from the theatre were regarded as not quite acceptable in polite society. While Garrick himself had been dead for fifty years when the club was founded, enlisting the memory of one of the nation's greatest actors was a mark of serious intent.

Of the founding members of the Garrick, the leading lights were Samuel Beazley, a prolific dramatist and the architect who was to be responsible for the rebuilding of the Lyceum theatre and James Winston, the independently wealthy manager of the Theatre Royal, Drury Lane from 1819-1826. The two men were a study in contrasts – the rakish Beazley whose erratic love life had produced several illegitimate children as compared to the ultra-respectable Winston. But together they had all the right connections.

An encouraging response from prospective members, including a fair sprinkling of the ruling class though, interestingly, relatively few actors, started a search for suitable premises. Since at this juncture there were insufficient funds for a purpose-built club, the choice fell on the conversion of Probatt's Family Hotel at 35, King Street between a plate glass warehouse and a draper's shop. A hard bargain was struck with the owner of the hotel who agreed reluctantly to a bargain price on condition that all the money was paid up front. With typical zest, Sam Beazley took on the task of converting the cobbled-together premises into a welcome home from home for gentlemen of leisure. As a founding member, Charles Mathews loaned a number of his theatrical paintings, later to be the nucleus of a permanent collection. The Club was opened with a mutton chop lunch on February 1st, 1832.

The Club's first historian, Percy Fitzgerald, writing in 1906, declared the Garrick to be a 'turning point in the social life and habits' of London. 'It was an attempt to give some correct and official shape to the old jovial tavern intercourse to which all rank had long been addicted, but which was just beginning to die out'. As if to embrace the wider theatrical community the Shakespeare sentiment 'All the World's a Stage', was adopted as the Club's crest.

In fairness, other well-patronised clubs such as the Athenaeum on Pall Mall, founded two years earlier than the Garrick, owed much to the coffee house tradition. Aiming for the cultural elite, the Athenaeum even had a Writer's Corner, a club within a club, reserved exclusively for its famous authors and dramatists. But the Garrick had the edge as a more informal, homelier club where actors, writers and artists could mingle with their patrons.

Not that it was trouble free. One of the dubious characters who slipped through the filtering of undesirables was Henry Addison, a retired army officer on half pay, described as a 'portly, flamboyant bon viveur with a well waxed moustache disposed to tell tall stories'. Granted membership by virtue of writing operettas and farces, Addison was shown the door after failing to pay his subscription. In 1849, he edited the first *Who's Who*, then simply an almanac and a list of public officials. Another early member was forced to resign when a housemaid accused him of stealing the soap.

Other infelicities were recorded by the humourist and clergyman, Richard Harris Barham whose notes on the strengths and weaknesses (mostly weaknesses) of his fellow members was kept under wraps until fifty years after his death. To modern eyes, Barham's observations are in no way startling but, in his own day, it might have caused discomfort to be known as the detractor of Thomas Gaspey, editor of *The Sunday Times* as 'a low-bred, vulgar man' or in describing John Forster, close friend and admirer of Dickens and his first biographer, as 'a low scribbler, without an atom of talent and totally unused to the society of gentlemen'.

Whatever the qualities, or lack of them, detected in the Garrick members there could be no question that the Club was off to a flying start with a substantial waiting list of candidates eager to join. Indeed, it was not long before there was talk of moving to larger premises. Leading the way was the growing contingent of lawyer members who favoured the Garrick for its proximity to the Inns of Court. The opportunity came with the clearing of slum property around Seven Dials to create a new street connecting Covent Garden to St Martin's Lane.

The planning, for what was known for convenience as New King Street, was the responsibility of Frederick Marrable, the chief architect for the Metropolitan Board of Works. Marrable was, at best, a safe pair of hands, with perhaps an exaggerated view of his own importance. Selected by the Garrick committee to create for them a clubhouse that was sufficiently imposing externally while providing convenience and comfort within, Marrable came up with an imposing Italianesque façade occupying most of one side of the street.

While Marrable was busy on the new Garrick, he fell out badly with the Metropolitan Board of Works over his remuneration. An increase that fell well short of his demand led to his resignation in February 1861. However, he continued with the Garrick as a freelance architect, completing the project on time and on budget. The move from the King Street premises was completed in September 1864. The Garrick took a chance on Marrable. As far as is known, no competitive designs were called for even though there were some who felt that an architect with more imagination might have been engaged. The gamble paid off.

As Club historian Geoffrey Wansell comments, along with 'a magnificent dining room...and...a noble staircase of carved oak... Marrable coped with the higgledy-piggledy nature of the back of the building with great skill and gave the new clubhouse the feeling of a small country house in the middle of theatre land – an atmosphere it has never lost.'

The inevitable grumbles were less about the building and more about the site with the attendant noise and smells of the Market. But occasional suggestions that the Garrick should move to the sedate club land of Pall Mall were rejected by the consensus who appreciated the bohemian touch provided by Covent Garden. As if to endorse the feeling of permanence, New King Street was renamed Garrick Street.

Eccentricity was endemic at the Garrick. It was certainly the hallmark of Charles Reade a writer who has gained classic status with his historical novel, *The Cloister and the Hearth*. Something of a loner, marginalised in male company by his dislike of wine and tobacco, he found companionship with his dog and a miscellany of small pets. His first London lodgings, he recalled, were 'alive with squirrels, who bolted up the curtains'. His dress was unconventional. Meeting him at the Garrick, a Colonel Hanley, who dressed smartly in military manner, was taken aback by Reade's appearance. 'He wore a large blue coat with brass buttons, and the widest trousers I ever saw on legs'. The journalist, Goldwin Smith, said of Reade, 'His behaviour was not less eccentric than his costume. We took him, in fact, to be almost crazy.' But also shrewd. A passion for collecting violins, seen as further proof of his idiosyncrasy, was in fact a paying business. The inspiration came on him during a continental tour when he discovered that old instruments were for sale at modest prices. In partnership with a Soho violin-maker, Reade launched on a buying spree. In a petition to the Treasury in 1848 protesting at the high rate of import duty on a consignment of violins, he detailed his enterprise.

> *To take off the bellies of every carcass except the Bass:*
> *to cut out the old Bass bars, which will not support the*
> *modern system of tuning a violin; to shape and glue new*
> *bass bars; to open and clean and glue all the cracks in*
> *those twenty carcasses and secure them with pieces; to*
> *shape and fit the necks to the scrolls and to the carcasses;*

to shape and fit the finger boards to the necks, to cut
and fit the bridge to each Instrument respectively; to
strengthen the bellies of one half of them inside with
pieces, carefully and laboriously; to string them up.

Far from being eccentric, the operation stands as a symbol of the Victorian entrepreneurial spirit.

Reade's breakthrough, *It is Never Too Late to Mend*, was published in 1856. The plot turns on a squire's villainous obsession with a younger woman that leads to her lover being sent to jail for a crime he did not commit. The notoriety attached to the book centred on Reade's revelations of the inhumane conditions of prison life, a subject on which he had made himself an expert.

He was equally punctilious in collecting evidence against the corrupt management of private asylums. In 1858, he campaigned in the correspondence columns of the press for a root and branch reform of 'Our Dark Places'. The controversy he aroused spurred him to write *Hard Cash*, a fictionalised onslaught on the abuse of the law and of the vague understanding of mental illness by families eager to put away unwanted relatives. Five years later, in *Foul Play*, Reade brought to bear his passion for justice on the racket of overloading ships with the intention of sinking them for the insurance money. Never free from controversy, Reade was quick to react to criticism with furious letters to newspapers. He was, said a journalist who had come under the lash, 'a literary fuse. You have only to touch him and he goes off.'

The contenders for top place in English letters at the time – Charles Dickens and Willian Makepeace Thackeray – were both Garrick members. They did not get on.

Dickens was irritated by Thackeray's 'eternal guffaw at all things' (he was a regular contributor to *Punch*) while Thackeray thought of Dickens as an idealist who failed to recognise the inevitability of inequality and injustice'. Dickens had more of the radical edge. In his journal *Household Words*, he spoke out against conditions in prisons, the inhumanity of workhouses, the poor standards of charity schools and allowing beggars to throng the streets. But a broad streak of conservatism in Dickens was revealed when he voiced his disgust at semi-nudity favoured by the Pre-Raphaelites and the sacrilege of Millais in portraying *Christ in the House of His Parents* (surely one of the greatest Victorian paintings). Dickens was opposed to public hangings but favoured harsh punishment for criminals.

Penny (or occasionally six penny) readings and recitations from literature came into vogue in the 1850s. Dickens was quick to help satisfy public demand. As one of the biggest names on the lecture circuit, he was able to command high fees and attract large audiences. Thackeray was no match. He dreaded public speaking and often lost his nerve at critical moments freezing in mid-sentence. While subsequently adopting the view that eminent writers should not cavort on stage for general amusement. That he summoned the courage to undertake a series of lectures and, like Dickens, to embark on an American tour was a measure of his determination to beat Dickens at his own game. He failed miserably.

The Garrick has enjoyed two colossal strokes of good fortune. The first was acquiring the theatrical works of art collected by Charles Mathews. At the height of his career in the early years of the nineteenth century when money was no object, Mathews began buying pictures at such a rate as to require the building of an art gallery as an extension to his home in north London.

Life for Mathews took a turn for the worse. After losing most of his wealth on ill-advised speculation, he was forced to offer his collection for sale. Hoping to find a buyer for his paintings as a single lot, he mounted an exhibition at the Queen's Bazaar in Oxford Street. It was a dismal failure with only a few items sold individually. An offer to sell the collection to the National Gallery also met with a rejection, an early example of the myopia of self-appointed art 'experts'.

Broken in health and spirit, Mathews died, aged 59, in 1835. Meanwhile, a few of his paintings were still on loan to the Garrick Club while it was at it King Street base. When the Club moved to it new premises, the stockbroker and founder member, John Rowland Durrant, floated the idea that the Garrick might acquire the entire theatrical collection, albeit at a knockdown price. With Durrant offering to put up the money, a deal was struck to clear the way for the Garrick to acquire the foundation of what has become 'the largest and most significant collection of British theatrical works of art'. Over the years many donations and purchases have enhanced the original collection so that now Mathews can be credited with only a quarter of the inventory. Several of the best paintings such as Johann Zoffany's *The Clandestine Marriage*, have been with the Club from the start.

The Garrick's second lucky break was to be left a quarter share of the royalties attached to the verse and stories for children by A. A. Milne. How this came about is a story in itself. A Club member from 1919, Milne considered himself a serious writer whose contribution to children's literature, notably *Winnie-the-Pooh* published in 1926 and *The House at Pooh Corner* two years later were but a side-line to his work for the stage. His bequest was thus less magnanimous than might at first be supposed.

As related in Geoffrey Wansell's history of the Garrick, 'it was estimated that the so-called Pooh royalties would bring in some £50,000 per annum' though they would take some years to reach that elevated level – in fact until the Disney Corporation decided to make Winnie-the-Pooh a worldwide 'brand' in the 1980s. In the end, Milne's 'Pooh' bequest brought in far more, literally millions of pounds, first in royalties and then in a lump sum payment from the Disney Corporation that capitalised the remaining years of royalty income and saw the Garrick receive a sum of almost £40 million in 2001. Ironically, Milne and his family were convinced that it would be his plays that would ensure fame and fortune. After Milne's death they were to reserve the royalties from those works to the family, yet they proved all but worthless in comparison. Only his adaptation of *Toad of Toad Hall* by fellow Garrick member Kenneth Grahame has survived.

The money flowing from Pooh came not a moment too soon for the Garrick. From the 1960s, the old established London clubs had been losing their appeal. Regarded by the younger generation, not without reason, as stuffy and hidebound, membership was in decline while standards suffered from rising costs and staff shortages. Until the Pooh royalties came on tap, the Garrick had been making ends meet by selling pictures off the walls and books from the library. Thanks to A. A. Milne, a major renovation was suddenly affordable. It took several years to complete but the Garrick can now boast one of the finest club houses in Britain and beyond. Moreover, funds were available to clean and restore the paintings which for too long had remained disguised under a veneer of tobacco smoke.

The Garrick has often been in the news. Why this should be so is hard to say. Other clubs of equal standing are rarely, if ever, in the public eye. The latest controversy has had to do with the admission of women as members. Tradition from Victorian times has dictated that prestigious clubs were men only. Equal rights has changed all that but the 'gentlemen's' clubs have been slow to adapt. It was only in 2024, after much internal anguish and wide press coverage, that the Garrick voted to admit women.

Of other contentious debates that have riven the normally placid Garrick, the most vigorously fought have turned on freedom of speech. Describing himself as a 'knock about' journalist, Malcom Muggeridge was, in fact, a well-informed maverick who specialised in bucking the trend. In October 1957, the *Saturday Evening Post* in New York carried an article in which Muggeridge put the question 'Does England really need a Queen?' Contrary to the hysterical follow-up stories in the British press, Muggeridge did not call for the abolition of the monarchy. His most telling criticism was of the Queen's exclusively upper-class entourage, 'a circumstance which makes them exceptionally incompetent'. He also took a knock at the BBC for its deferential reporting on royal matters. All fair comment, one would have thought. Not for the old stagers at the Garrick who called for Muggeridge's expulsion for 'conduct unbecoming to a gentleman'. Their case was strengthened by the publication of the offending article to coincide with the Queen's official visit to Washington. After further public wrangling the fuss subsided only to resurface when in February 1964, Muggeridge appeared on an American television chat show declaring that the British monarchy had 'all the ingredients of a soap opera', adding, 'The English are getting bored with their monarchy ... the public realise the monarchy has become over-exposed. I think it is coming to an end'.

It was all carried off at a jokey level, the chat show host winding up by telling viewers, 'Gee, I hope they don't behead him. He's going back to Britain tonight.'

The British press was quick to respond, with the *Sunday Express* setting the tone by denouncing Muggeridge's comments as 'sordid and shabby'. The Garrick was not far behind. The protests were led by Sir Laurence Rivers Dunne, Chief Metropolitan Magistrate, whose outpourings of anger and disgust brought a whole new meaning to bigotry.

A great believer in self-control, moral duty and the firm enforcement of the law, he called for longer prison sentences and the reintroduction of birching for young offenders while opposing the abolition of capital punishment. In the ideal world of Rivers Dunne, National Health Service (NHS) expenditure on spectacles, false teeth and wigs would be diverted to fund sports clubs and playing fields to encourage urban youths to adopt manly pursuits. The rise in vice crime he blamed on the 'multitude of coloured men now entering this country'. It comes as no surprise that Rivers Dunne was obsessed by homosexuality, though he took heart from the decline in the 'old unholy traffic between soldiers of the Guards and Household Cavalry and perverts in the Royal Parks' which he credited to 'the ranks no longer wearing tight overalls off duty'. Well may it have been said by the royals, with friends like this who needs enemies?

Though Muggeridge had his free speech defenders at the Garrick, he did not put up much of a fight. Wearing the martyrs' crown, he resigned from the Club while protesting his inalienable right 'to say whatever I like about anything anywhere'.

8

Charles Dickens, unknown; William Makepeace Thackeray by
Sir John Gilbert RA, PRWS; Edmund Yates, by Frederick Sem;
all courtesy of the Garrick Club, London

The Garrick Affair

*Rivalry between Dickens and Thackeray; Marital
discord; Edmund Yates and gossip journalism;
Expulsion of Yates from the Garrick Club and
aftermath.*

Another newsworthy controversy that disrupted the even tenor
of Garrick life was the row between Charles Dickens and William
Makepeace Thackeray.

With hindsight, a falling out was inevitable. Though highly talented and successful, they were also self-centred, almost narcissistic, acutely sensitive and quick to blame others when things did not go their way. They resented criticism and feared exposure of their failings.

While their joint output was impressive, Dickens had the edge as a man of business and as a talent-spotter who brought on young writers and pioneered book publishing by serialisation. Thackeray took longer to get into his stride. Having built a reputation as a sharp observer with his travel writing, *Vanity Fair*, a powerful dissection of Victorian society, was published in a decade after Pickwick. His cynical take on high society was seen as something of an antidote to Dickens's brand of sentimentality. The contrast highlighted the rivalry between the two authors. Relations were distantly cordial; they were rarely seen in the same room.

Dickens and Thackeray did have one thing in common. Both treated their wives abominably and both refused to acknowledge any part of the blame for their failed marriages. Thackeray's choice of life partner was Isabella Shawe, a small and shy 18-year-old who lived in Paris with her widowed mother, a mean and embittered woman who was hoping for something better for her daughter than marriage to a scribbler with no fixed prospects. A war of attrition with Mrs Shawe ended with a pyrrhic victory for Thackeray. He married his 'nice, simple, girlish girl' in August 1836.

Almost immediately, he was complaining that his wife was lazy, cold and undemonstrative. While her mother sniped from the side lines, it apparently never occurred to her or Thackeray that the over-protected Isabella needed more than usual support to cope with her new life. A period of decline accelerated with post-natal depression brought on by the birth of Minnie, their third child, in 1840.

After three years of marriage and three daughters (one died in infancy) Thackeray had had enough of domesticity. Family duties were farmed out to his mother, who was to have virtually sole care of the children for six years. Thackeray found his consolation and inspiration in male company. For public consumption he longed for 'a lodge in some vast wilderness' where he could write in peace. The reality was that he needed people, preferably his admirers around him.

Dickens was similarly disillusioned with family life. Having married the 'pretty and accomplished' Catherine Hogarth, the 19-year-old daughter of the editor of the *Evening Chronicle*, in April 1836, the relationship soured when Catherine's younger sister Mary joined the household. Dickens was besotted with a child virgin, a tendency that was to recur with dramatic consequences twenty years later. When Mary died suddenly after a short illness, Dickens was so devastated he was unable to work, unique in his busy career. Like Thackeray, Dickens did not get on with his mother-in-law whom he accused of being interfering, grasping and domineering. Mrs Hogarth was undoubtedly a factor in turning him against Catherine.

In 1842 when Dickens took Catherine on his first trip to America, her sister, Georgina was left in charge of the children. Remaining with the household until Dickens's death in 1870,

Georgina was to play a major role in the scandal that was to break when Dickens decided to end his marriage. But long before then Dickens was chafing against domesticity, complaining that with Catherine pregnant for most of the time (hardly her fault), his house was 'nothing but a hospital ward'. Catherine's post-natal depression was intensified by giddiness and migraines. Dickens had time for everything except for giving support to his wife.

Thackeray was the ultimate club man. He was a member of the Reform, where he had his own desk, and of the Athenaeum where he made use of the extensive library. But his favourite was the bohemian Garrick. A heavy eater and drinker, Thackeray took delight in the lively male camaraderie of smoke-filled rooms. He was equally at home in less reputable establishments such as Evans's Supper Rooms in Covent Garden and The Deanery, a smoking den in the back parlour of a tavern near St Paul's. He was also a regular at the weekly gatherings around the *Punch* table where the conversation was far riper than the articles that appeared in the journal.

By contrast, Dickens as much as Thackeray was drawn to all-male company. He preferred to be with fellow writers in small groups. With his friends John Forster and the popular novelist, Harrison Ainsworth, he set up the Trio Club with just themselves as members. Unlike Thackeray, Dickens drank and ate very little. But more to the point, Dickens was confident enough not to need the approval of society grandees. Thackeray was ever seeking social position, his jealousy of Dickens revealed in his comment that his rival was 'not quite a gentleman'.

A major crisis in Thackeray's life came in 1840 when he took his family to Ireland for what was supposed to be a convalescent holiday for Isabella. On board the paddle-steamer Jupiter from London to Cork, she threw herself over the side and was in the water for twenty minutes before being rescued.

Given the then limited understanding of mental illness it is an open question as to what Thackeray could have done to restore his family to normal life. But he did not even try. Instead, having inspected an asylum, and found it wanting or, more probably, too expensive, Thackeray decided to put his wife into the care of Mrs Bakewell and her daughter at their house in Camberwell. This cost him £2 a week.

Having disposed of his troublesome wife, Thackeray moved on to write his first big successes, *The Snobs of England* and *Vanity Fair*. While his earnings increased substantially, there was no extra money for Isabella whose upkeep remained at an annual £104.

Dining out almost every night, Thackeray lived a full bucolic life. Garrulous by nature, he covered every subject under the sun but never mentioned his wife. Nor did he visit her or allow the children to do so. Any guilt he might have felt was assuaged by reports from Mrs Bakewell 'a most excellent worthy woman' that Isabella was well and cheerful.

Thackeray's mid-life crisis was a rich source of gossip and rumour. His friendship with Charlotte Brontë gave traction to hearsay that the plot of *Jane Eyre*, in which the heroine discovers that her prospective husband had a mad wife, was based on knowledge of Thackeray's troubles. Support for this notion came in the second edition of *Jane Eyre* which was dedicated to Thackeray. That there was no truth in the rumour was no deterrent to another wild accusation, that Thackeray had seduced his children's governess, a story embroidered by the claim that Currer Bell, aka Charlotte Brontë, had been that same governess.

Thackeray was naturally furious when the story was fed back to him. But while he inveighed against gossip that impugned base motives, others noted that what he found intolerable he was quite ready to inflict on others. Quarrels where he usually ended up having to apologise were a regular feature of his life.

When the writer Douglas Jerrold died suddenly, leaving nothing in the bank, Dickens moved quickly to help support his family. A melodrama, *The Frozen Deep* by Wilkie Collins, was chosen for money-raising performances round the country. A largely amateur cast led by Dickens, was bolstered by professional actors. These included Eleanor Ternan and her two daughters, Ellen and Maria. In his stage role, Dickens, as the older man, had to fall in love with Ellen and shower her with jewellery. Before long, fiction was to be made real.

Ellen was 18 when Dickens first met her, only slightly older than his daughter Katey. Dickens was 45, showing signs of premature aging but with his personality undiminished. He found in Ellen a kindred soul. Reviving memories of his close relationship with his young sister-in-law Mary, Dickens was once again in thrall to pubescent innocence. Though not a great actress, Ellen was attractive with a strong presence. She knew enough of literature and the theatre to talk to Dickens on equal terms. The great man was smitten.

Dickens's affair with Ellen Ternan had a traumatic effect on his judgement. As a public figure he was terrified of exposure to the stern and unforgiving gaze of his middle class following. Catherine, his wife, a more assertive character than is often assumed, stoked up the drama. A favourite anecdote, circulated by Thackeray and others, was of Catherine opening a package from a London jeweller to find a gold bracelet intended for Ellen. As is the way with gossip, no one thought to ask why, if Catherine's story was true, Dickens had chosen to have the bracelet delivered to his home. The snippet was too good to be disbelieved.

For all practical purposes, the marriage ended when Catherine and her eldest son, Charley, moved out of the marital home. Dickens never spoke to her again. In increasingly desperate efforts to justify himself, Dickens tried to blacken Catherine's character, claiming that his wife acted coldly towards the children who felt no affection for her which was patently untrue.

A superficial reading of the recently enacted Divorce Bill appeared to open the possibility of divorce based on Dickens's adultery. But the legislation was inequitable. While a man could file for divorce on grounds of adultery alone, a woman had to prove additional wrongdoing. Evidence of cruelty would suffice but against Dickens this would be hard to prove. However, there was another, far more insidious charge, that might be levelled against him.

The loyalty of Georgina, Dickens's sister-in-law, could be construed as a much closer relationship. Under the law, this amounted to incest, a crime as well as grounds for divorce. There were those who were only too happy to believe the gossip heard, as one antagonistic correspondent put it, 'at every corner of every street and in every social circle'. Dickens was particularly incensed by suggestions that Ellen Ternan was his mistress. He retaliated with an open letter castigating the 'wicked persons' who had instigated the rumours and declaring Ellen, though without naming her, as 'innocent and pure ... as my own two daughters'. A likely story! was the general reaction.

In the same letter, Dickens made the highly contentious claim that Catherine laboured under a 'mental disorder' which made her unfit as a wife and mother. Undeterred by warnings, he authorised his letter to be shown to 'anyone who wishes to do me right, or to anyone who may have been misled into doing me wrong'. The contents were duly revealed to a journalist who wrote up the story for the *New York Times*. It was not long before the British press weighed in.

It has been said that Dickens was devastated by the circulation of what was now known as the 'violated letter'. The likelihood is that, naively, Dickens reckoned on his public statement putting a stop to idle gossip. But with all his experience of popular journalism, it should not have come as a surprise that it had the reverse effect.

Inevitably, Thackeray was drawn into the affair. Recalling the adage about the pot and the kettle, he sided with Catherine on the grounds that after 22 years of marriage she deserved better. Taking umbrage, Dickens was further enraged when it was fed back to him that in a Garrick conversation, Thackeray had revealed the affair with Ellen Ternan. In a desperate attempt at self-vindication, Dickens circulated a strong denial of 'lately whispered rumours' telling of his domestic troubles. That he provided no details was like gold dust to the gossip mongers. In June 1858, Catherine agreed to the terms of separation. Her allowance was to be £600 a year, this at a time when Dickens was bringing in £10,000.

After simmering for so many years, the ill feeling between Dickens and Thackeray boiled over in what became known as the Garrick Affair.

It started in the summer of 1858 with an article by Edmund Yates, one of Dickens's young protégés, who was beginning to make his way in the new and highly competitive world of society journalism. His chief source of income was a regular column called 'Lounger at the Clubs' for the *Illustrated Times* in which he profiled fellow-writers, theatrical people and artists. His claim to insider knowledge, either real or pretended, angered those who resented the flippant style adopted by Yates. In 1856 he was in serious trouble in the wake of the Palmer murder trial for suggesting, on the say-so of a 'usually accurate source', that Palmer had bought stable secrets from employees of Lord Derby, the doyen of the racing fraternity. Threatened with a prosecution for libel, Yates got off with a grovelling apology.

More trouble came his way when he profiled Thackeray as a 'literary celebrity' in a new weekly penny magazine called *Town Talk*. While praising Thackeray as a 'great genius', he accused him 'of a want of heart in all he writes', concluding 'that his success is on the wane'. If Yates was guilty of anything, it was bad timing. In the previous week's issue of *Town Talk*, he had heaped praise on Dickens as he appeared at his public readings, a performer with eyes 'flashing with extraordinary brilliancy' and a 'deep and sonorous' voice 'capable of exquisite modulation and of expressing the deepest feeling'.

Thackeray bridled at what he took to be a deliberately malicious comparison of talents, not to mention the implication that he was not universally admired. As his resentment built up, he took it into his head that while there was no mention of any club in the *Town Talk* article, Yates had based his observations on what he had heard in conversations at the Garrick. To add fuel to his anger, he was convinced that it was Yates who had fed back to Dickens his comments about Ellen Ternan. He demanded an apology.

After consulting Dickens, who, predictably, saw no reason for Yates to backtrack, he sent Thackeray a cold rebuttal of a 'curiously bitter outburst of personal feeling'. The result was to incite Thackeray to further action. He now decided to refer the dispute to the Garrick committee asking whether the 'practice of publishing such articles ... will not be fatal to the comfort of the Club and is not intolerable in a Society of Gentlemen'.

The Club sided with Thackeray. This was hardly surprising given that for Thackeray the Garrick was a home from home where he was frequently to be found while Dickens was rarely to be seen on the premises. Yates was told to apologise or to face expulsion. The committee added that Yates had been unfortunate in his choice of advisers. This was too much for Dickens who resigned from the committee. His place was taken by a close friend of Thackeray.

When Yates refused to concede, a special general meeting of the club supported the committee. It was noted that the club divided on class lines with most of the older, aristocratic members siding with Thackeray leaving Yates and Dickens with a smaller faction of young Bohemians. Given the social and literary climate, expulsion from one's club was a serious business. To the humiliation piled on Yates was added the risk of social ostracism. Hoping to reverse the decision, Yates took legal advice but was deterred by the cost of an action.

Though Thackeray was able to claim outright victory, in the longer term he was the loser. Criticised in the press for excessive sensitivity, he took the blame for what was now an open rift with Dickens. In November, Dickens suggested 'some kind of mediation' that would allow for Yates to regain Garrick membership. If that proved to be impossible, wrote Dickens, he urged that related correspondence should be burned. Instead, Thackeray handed over the letter to the Garrick committee, confirming suspicions that it was not so much Yates as Dickens himself who was counted as the enemy.

It was not until 1863, five years after the climax of the Garrick Affair, that the two men managed to shake hands, some say on the steps of the Athenaeum, others that the encounter was at Drury Lane Theatre. In any event, neither said a word. There was no further opportunity for a reconciliation. Overweight and short of breath, Thackeray died on Christmas Eve 1863, aged 52, of a burst blood vessel in the brain.

But Dickens continued with his pretence of domestic respectability. Though Ellen was recognised in his will, their affair remained closed to the outside world. It was Victorian hypocrisy at its worst.

Like Thackeray, Dickens died young. He was only 58 at his death in 1870. Some of his best work – *A Tale of Two Cities, Great Expectations* and *Our Mutual Friend* – were published in his last decade.

As for Yates, he went on to an eventful journalistic career which included bankruptcy caused by unwise theatrical investment and a conviction for criminal libel which led to a heavy fine and four months in prison. He kept in with Dickens seeing him regularly up to the last weeks of Dickens's life. After his expulsion from the Garrick, Yates was elected to the Carlton.

9

Cover of the Christmas 1922 edition of the magazine featuring
Sherlock Holmes and P.G. Wodehouse

'Let's All Go Down the Strand'

*Strand palaces; Opening of Charing Cross station; The
Adams Brothers and the Adelphi Terrace; The Royal
Society of Arts; Coutts Bank; Angela Burdett-Coutts,
'Queen of the Poor': Exeter Hall; the Royal Courts of
Justice; Twinings.*

Strand was once a street of palaces. For the rich and powerful, the
chief attraction was the proximity of the Thames, Strand or, in old
English strond, being literally the bank of a river. While providing the easiest and fastest travel between the City and the centre
of government at Westminster, Strand was also an attractive place
to live. As recorded by a German visitor to London in 1602, the
view south from Strand was of spacious gardens sloping down to
the water's edge where bystanders could watch the fishermen casting their nets while cargo vessels from 'almost every corner of the
world…come almost up to the city to which they convey goods
and receive and take away others in exchange'.

Particular note was taken of the many swans, 'so tame that you
can almost touch them, though it is forbidden on pain of corporal
punishment in any way to injure a swan, for Royalty has them
plucked every year, in order to have their down for court-use.'

The downside was a tidal sewer that carried raw sewage out
to sea but too often, at high tide, bringing it back again. Nor was
Strand itself an advertisement for gentility. As late as 1756, a

French visitor complained that 'the middle of the road was garnished with a thick muddy liquid three or four inches deep so that pedestrians were bemired from head to foot... and the centre kennel was constantly stopped up because...lazy servants threw offal and dust and rubbish into it...the heavy overhanging signboards of houses and taverns...were wont to fall on pedestrians' heads in very bad weather'.

This was a far cry from the days when Peter of Savoy, uncle of the wife of Henry III, built his palace between the Thames and Strand on land now occupied by the Savoy hotel and theatre. The palace and all its contents were destroyed in 1381 when the peasantry rose up in revolt against what was regarded as onerous taxation.

The only reminder now of the royal presence is the Savoy Chapel, originally part of accommodation for one hundred 'poor and needy men' founded by Henry VII. Completed in 1515, the Savoy Chapel suffered damage and neglect over the centuries but is now fully restored with a gloriously coloured ceiling modelled on the original Tudor ceiling but actually dating from 1843 after a fire. As part of the Duchy of Lancaster, the Chapel remains Crown property and was inaugurated as the Chapel Royal in 2016. A fine stained glass window commemorates the 2012 diamond jubilee of Queen Elizabeth II.

All the great houses have gone, though they retain a ghostly presence in the streets named after their occupants, such as Essex Street on the site of what in pre-Reformation days was the palace of the Bishops of Exeter and subsequently the home of the

Earls of Essex. The most splendid of Strand mansions was York House, briefly the residence of the Archbishops of York before its proximity to Whitehall and the royal palace marked it out as the official residence of the Lord Keeper of the Great Seal, a royal appointment equal and often joined to that of Lord Chancellor.

In London's hall of fame, a high ranking goes to the philosopher and statesman, Francis Bacon, who was born in York House on January 22nd, 1561. A contemporary records 'the courtyard and great gates opening to the street; the main front, with its turrets, facing the river'. The garden was 'of unusual size and splendour' commanding a view of the river 'as far east as London Bridge', adding 'all the gay river life swept past the lawn'.

Attorney General and Lord Chancellor of England under James I, Bacon was fiercely intellectual, an advocate of scientific observation and analysis to establish objective truths instead of relying on dogma handed down by the ancients. He spoke out for religious toleration and for an end to feudal privilege.

When Bacon stayed at York House after the death of his father he incurred the jealousy of George Villiers, Duke of Buckingham, a favourite of James I whose services to the crown extended to sharing the regal bed. Having gained possession of York House, forcing Bacon to find alternative accommodation, Buckingham set about demolishing the mansion to create an even grander house where he could display his collection of paintings including nineteen by Titian and thirteen by Rubens. With Inigo Jones appointed as architect the work proceeded slowly. In fact, it was never finished and what was extant was ordered to be pulled down by the second Duke who wanted the land for speculative housing. All that remains of York House is the magnificent Water Gate, designed by Inigo Jones, now marooned, as it were, on the Embankment, itself the product of land reclamation.

Family connections are recorded in street names such as Buckingham Street, Duke Street, George Court and Villiers Street. When he was Secretary of the Admiralty, the diarist Samuel Pepys lived and worked at No.14 Buckingham Street from 1679 to 1688. A century later, Samuel Taylor Coleridge wrote his verse narrative *The Rime of the Ancient Mariner* at No. 21.

But the strongest literary tie-in is with Charles Dickens who, as a cub reporter on the *Morning Chronicle*, lived at No. 15 where he taught himself shorthand and wrote his first fiction, a short story *A Dinner at Poplar Walk*; described by his biographer Peter Ackroyd as 'a light sketch concerning the misadventures which happened when families pursue putative legacies with too much earnestness'. Dickens was immoderately proud when the story was published in the *Monthly Magazine* though this grand-sounding periodical did not pay him for his contribution, nor, indeed for eight more of his stories accepted for publication. Buckingham Street was later to figure in *David Copperfield*, a semi-autobiographical novel, serialised in 1849 and published as a book a year later.

Somerset House gives every appearance of having once been a palace. While Edward Seymour, 1st Duke of Somerset, had every intention of building a residence fit for the all-powerful Protector of England during the minority of Edward VI, he failed to realise his dream before he was forced from power and executed.

Somerset House as we know it dates from the mid-eighteenth century when the site was cleared to allow for a 'national building' to house public bodies such as The Salt Office, The Stamp Office, The Tax Office and The Navy Office.

Technically Crown property, it was also used for state functions and for accommodating visiting dignitaries. The original south wing, finished in 1786, gave direct access to the Thames until the building of the Thames embankment in the 1840s. The focal point of Somerset House then shifted to the Palladian style north wing with the west and east wings occupied by the Royal Academy, albeit for a short time, and by the Royal Society and the Society of Antiquarians. Within living memory, Somerset House provided the rather grand setting for the Inland Revenue and the Registrar General of Births, Marriages and Deaths with the quadrangle serving as a parking lot.

Today, the restored Somerset House has been redeveloped as offices for enterprises with a cultural bent while in the north wing is the Courtauld Gallery with its magnificent collection of impressionist and old master paintings. In winter, the courtyard is transformed into an open-air ice rink.

At the other end of Strand, close to Trafalgar Square, Charing Cross rail station, fronted by the Charing Cross Hotel, commands the scene. The wonder is that the station was ever built. The South Eastern Railway with lines running into London Bridge lobbied for a terminus on the north side of the Thames. This made no real sense in planning. For one thing, it spelt the end of the popular Hungerford Market which put yet more pressure on the already overloaded Covent Garden. Then again, with the expected increase in commuter traffic as London expanded to the south, the construction of additional lines across the Thames would be costly and labour intensive. Notwithstanding the objections, Parliamentary permission for the new station was granted in August 1859. Five years later, the first trains steamed into Charing Cross. The Renaissance style Charing Cross Hotel with its 250 bedrooms on seven floors, was immediately popular, not least because until Victoria Station took on the role, Charing Cross was the terminus for boat trains to the Continent.

A ninety-room annex opened in 1878. Further changes came in the mid-1950s when the distinctive and widely-admired Mansard roof, with sloping ends on four sides, was removed to add an additional floor. The pleasing aesthetic of the building was irretrievably lost. In the forecourt of Charing Cross is a replica of the last of twelve Eleanor Crosses, erected in 1290 to mark the route of the funeral cortège for Eleanor, wife of Edward I.

Close by Charing Cross and below Strand is a small district known as Adelphi comprising John Adam Street, Robert Street and Adam Street, all named after the Adams brothers who were responsible for the Adelphi Terrace, a Thames-side residency of twenty four neo-classical houses built between 1768 and 1772.

One of the earliest occupants was the actor David Garrick, then at the height of his fame and fortune. Having lived for twenty-two years at 27 Southampton Street, he required a home that measured up to his celebrity. That he found it in Adelphi Terrace was partly as result of his friendship with the Adams brothers who had worked for him at his country villa at Hampton-on-Thames and partly his own family associations with the location since it was here, thirty years earlier, that he and his brother had established their wine vaults. Commissioned to fit out the house, Thomas Chippendale, London's premier furniture maker, was given a liberal budget to allow even for hung wallpaper imported from China by the East India Company. On March 15th, 1772, a team of Chippendale labourers hauled thirty horse-loads of 'sundry goods' from Southampton Street to the Adelphi. The cost was entered at one shilling per load. Garrick reported to a friend that his wife 'is almost killed with fatigue'.

Garrick had some illustrious neighbours. Topham Beauclerk, at No. 3, was the grandson of Charles II and Nell Gwyn. Dr John Turton, at No. 7, had recently been appointed physician to the Queen's Household. Another neighbour was Henry Hoare, nephew and heir of the head of the banking house of that name. Robert Adam himself lived at No. 4. Garrick was next door at No. 5.

With twenty-four rooms to furnish, Chippendale was kept busy. For the drawing room alone he provided a marble chimney-piece, a ceiling painted by the Italian artist Antonio Zucchi to represent Venus admired by the Graces in a cloudscape of pink and blue, two Pembroke tables, three commodes, two large armchairs with matching sofa and twelve 'Cabriole' armchairs. The fringed curtains were of green silk damask, and there were three large green Venetian sun blinds. For the dining room, all of mahogany, he made a sideboard, two pedestals (one to contain bottles, the other fitted as a plate-warmer), a table and twelve parlour chairs with morocco-leather seats. A necessary utilitarian touch in the pillared hall were sixteen canvas fire bags.

The Chippendale accounts (he was a meticulous book keeper) show that the final tally for furnishing Garrick's new home was close to one thousand pounds (around £250,000 today). In refusing a loan to his sister, Garrick moaned, 'All my ready money is exhausted'.

Moving into the twentieth century, one of the most intriguing residents of Adelphi Terrace was James Barrie who, like his fictional alter ego, Peter Pan, was a little boy who never grew up. He once said 'Nothing that happens after we are twelve matters very much' and he was not joking. He wrote short stories, novels and plays, taking his inspiration from the world of make-believe.

In *Dear Brutus*, a play still worthy of revival, a house party of guests, unhappy in their lives, get their chance to start again. But nothing changes. The point of the play is to show, by fantasy, that if we could relive our lives we would still make the same mistakes. *The Admiral Crichton*, another Barrie perennial, is based on the same pessimistic premise – that while circumstances change, the essentials, in this case the social hierarchy, endure. It shouldn't be so, says Barrie, but that's the way it is.

Barrie's devotion to fantasy reached its creative peak with *Peter Pan*, a fairy story with a modern hero that could have been Barrie himself in his ideal world. The inspiration for *Peter Pan* came from Barrie's relationship with the Llewelyn Davies's and their five sons who knew him as Uncle Jim. The play began to take shape in a Christmas entertainment he put together for the boys.

Barrie's passion for male juveniles, though highly suspect by to-day's standards, was almost certainly innocent. Sex simply did not interest Barrie. A bachelor by temperament, it is doubtful that his unhappy marriage to an actress was ever consummated, though his wife was desperate for children.

Soon afterwards, Barrie's life began to fall apart. It was after his divorce in 1909 that he moved to a flat at No. 3 Adelphi Terrace. Meanwhile, tragedy overtook the Llewelyn Davies family. After the parents died within three years of each other, Barrie took on the responsibility for their offspring. But the fantasy of an idyllic bond cracked under the weight of events. One of the boys died in action in 1915, a second drowned in a likely suicide pact with his lover in 1921. Twenty years after Barrie's death in 1937, Peter Llewelyn Davies threw himself under a train.

Late in life Barrie became reclusive, and on rare occasions that he dined with friends had little to contribute. In a story that made the rounds, Barrie was at a dinner party where he sat next to a woman who shared his antipathy to idle chat. Barrie made a brave effort to communicate. 'Have you ever been to China?' he asked the woman. 'No,' said the woman. After a long silence, she said, 'Have you?' 'No,' said Barrie. And that was that.

Determined to draw Barrie out of his shell, the dramatist R.C. Sherriff, whose first plays were modelled on Barrie's work, invited himself to tea. Sherriff thought Adelphi Terrace a 'desolate and barren' place where the lower floors were occupied by offices. The door to the flat was opened by a small man ('I hadn't known how short he was – almost a dwarf') who led the way into a 'big, gaunt living room, furnished in an off-hand sort of way as if from time to time he had picked up things that took his fancy without caring whether they would go together'. The setting was certainly not conducive to lively discourse.

> *There was a long, uncomfortable looking wooden bench*
> *before the fire, and behind it a table laid out for tea,*
> *with a chair beside it. There was a large home-made*
> *cake and a plate of bread and butter, cut rather thick. ...*
> *it was an awkward arrangement from the social point of*
> *view because my chair beside the tea-table was behind*
> *the wooden bench, and all I could see of Barrie was*
> *the top of his head. It wasn't easy to talk to him to his*
> *face. Far less to the top of his head. He pushed the little*
> *cushion behind his neck, settled down and lapsed into*
> *silence.*

While coping with an unappetising slice of cake, Sherriff began to wonder if his host, 'so completely still and silent', had died. Since there was no telephone, he imagined dashing out of the flat to find a policeman. He was about to check the breathing when Barrie stirred.

> *He sat up, stared into the fire, and pulled an old charred*
> *pipe out of his pocket. He filled and lit it, puffed out*
> *clouds of smoke, and began to cough as if it were choking*
> *him. For a little while I could scarcely see him for smoke.*
> *When it had cleared away he looked at me as if he'd*

forgotten I was there, and said, 'I expect you'll want to be going'.

He took me into the outside hall, helped me on with my Burberry coat and gave me his hat.

'I think this is yours,' I said.

He looked at it in puzzled surprise, then eagerly took it back and hung it carefully on a peg. 'No,' he said, 'you mustn't have that!' ... I said goodbye and went down the stairs. The offices below were closed. Everybody had gone home. I wondered what Barrie would do for the rest of the long lonely night.

Adelphi Terrace was demolished in the 1930s to be replaced by the vast Art Deco block which reminded one critic of totalitarian architecture – monumental, featureless and forbidding.

Thankfully, much of the resplendent John Adam Street was saved by the Royal Society of Arts which occupies five of the houses. The RSA, or to give it its full name, The Royal Society for the Encouragement of Arts, Manufacture and Commerce, was founded in 1754 at a meeting of like-minded innovators at Rawthmell's Coffee House in Henrietta Street. Their high flown mission was 'to embolden enterprise, enlarge science, refine art, improve our manufacturers and extend our commerce' along with alleviating poverty and securing full employment. A royal charter was granted in 1847 and the 'royal' appellation added in 1908.

It was at the RSA that the fashion for exhibitions evolved, initially for painters to display their canvases, but after the creation of the Royal Academy, chiefly for manufacturers to promote their latest products. Ever more ambitious projects led to the Great Exhibition of 1851, the proudest moment in the RSA's history, though chief credit for the success of the enterprise must go to its royal sponsor, Prince Albert, who made of it a ringing proclamation of British commercial leadership.

The Great Exhibition set a standard, adopted by all the successor trade exhibitions in Britain, France and the United States, of spectacular displays (the Crystal Palace, built with a single glass and iron framework and covering 19 acres, was alone worth the price of admission) which sought to 'improve the taste of the middle classes, to inform manufacturer about mechanical improvements and to morally educate the working class'.

A century on, the RSA was active in initiating and promoting the 1951 Festival of Britain to give the country a much-needed boost after the wartime misery and austerity that followed. Transforming the derelict site on the south bank of the Thames, the Festival attracted over eight million visitors. The only surviving building is the Festival Hall, originally to be called The People's Palace until wiser counsel prevailed.

At the other side of Strand from Charing Cross is Bedford Street once favoured by drapers, mercers and lacemen after the 1666 Great Fire persuaded them to move beyond the old city boundaries. The Charing Cross Hospital, one of eight of London's casualty hospitals, moved from Villiers Street to Bedford Street in

1831. It stayed there until 1973 when it migrated to Hammersmith while still, confusingly, retaining Charing Cross in its name.

A great sprawl of a building, all white tiling and echoing corridors, the old hospital had a medical school with students performing minor operations. In my own student days at the London School of Economics I took advantage of the walk-in facility to have an unsightly cyst removed from my forehead. I was given over to a medical trainee of about my own age. Supervised by a short-tempered surgeon, he showed signs of nervousness that spread to the patient. With a mask over my face, I was unable to witness what was going on but was reassured by a kindly nurse who made light of a tray of instruments crashing to the floor. 'No need to worry', the nurse told me, 'that was just a doctor fainting at the sight of blood'.

Until it moved its office to the other end of Strand, Bedford Street was home to that misery guts organisation, the Lord's Day Observance Society which campaigned for Sunday to be made as boring as humanly possible, with no work, no sports, no newspapers and most definitely no form of live entertainment. In my time, the Society's secretary boasted that he never cleaned his shoes on the day of rest and would not permit his wife to iron a shirt. As a measure of its power as a lobby for outmoded conventions, in 1950 a Parliamentary bill to relax the rules on Sunday entertainment was defeated in the House of Commons by 281 votes to 57. Thankfully, we have moved on from Victorian parochialism.

Opposite Charing Cross Station is Coutts Bank. With its reputation for sound finance secured in the nineteenth century by its then sole proprietor, Thomas Coutts, the bank attracted a clientele from the commercial and social elite. While the banker conveyed to his ever-expanding roster of aristocratic clients an image of sober gravity, he was by no means cast in the conventional mould. Instead of marrying into the clan that provided him with his substantial income, he had chosen as his wife the daughter of a Lancashire farmer who had worked for his brother as a housemaid. She had presented him with three daughters.

However, Coutts was not the stay-at-home type. In his later years, his wandering eye fastened on an actress famed more for her beauty than for stage talents. Her name was Harriot Mellon. The child of a broken marriage, Harriot started her career as a strolling player, visiting booths and barns in Lancashire and Yorkshire. Spotted by Richard Brinsley Sheridan, she joined the cast of his comedy *The Rivals* at Drury Lane to play uncredited bit parts. Advancing to leading roles, she attracted a bevy of wealthy admirers. At their head was Thomas Coutts.

While their relationship was close, Coutts had no intention of breaking up the family home. It was not until his wife died in 1814 that he made a formal proposal. He was then eighty. The couple had seven contented years before Harriot came into an inheritance of close on a million pounds and a house looking out on Piccadilly from Stratton Street. Though middle aged, she was still turning heads, her appeal now enhanced by her income. Of the many offers of marriage, there was only one she took seriously, that of William Aubrey de Vere Beauclerk, 9th Duke of St Albans. It was said, cynically, to be an ideal match; Harriot liked the idea of being a duchess while her suitor was in urgent need of funds. The chief gift to the gossip mongers, however, was the difference in ages. Harriot was twice as old as her husband. Yet by all accounts, it was a happy marriage. It ended after ten years with Harriot's death. Remarkably, given the dominant male role sanctified by law, Harriot had secured a marriage settlement that had left her in sole control of her fortune which had continued to grow.

Even more remarkably, after a generous allowance for the Duke, she left everything to the youngest of the grand-daughters of Thomas Coutts. A deeply religious, socially withdrawn young lady, Angela Burdett-Coutts (she had changed her surname to meet the terms of her grandmother's will) was now enormously rich. Philanthropy was her first love. In addition to model housing at affordable rents, she built two churches and endowed church schools. A friend of Florence Nightingale, she paid for a drying machine to be sent to the Crimea so that soldiers would not have to wear wet clothes. A co-founder of the London Society for the Protection of Cruelty to Children, she was also, more improbably, the first patron, later President, of the British Goat Society. The owner of several goats, she was convinced of the healthy properties of goat's milk.

Angela's philanthropic efforts were not all successful. One of her failures, which might have put up warning signals to those intent on modernising Covent Garden, was the purpose-built Columbia Market in London's East End. This Gothic pile, designed to meet the highest standards of hygiene, was spurned by street traders who anticipated the officious attention of health inspectors and other busy-bodies intent on making life difficult.

In 1871 Angela was created Baroness Burdett-Coutts. It was an honour she was not sure she deserved. Of more value to her was the title bestowed on her by the East End, the Queen of the Poor.

In the autumn of her life, Angela sprang a surprise on her friends and admirers by following the example of her step-grand-mother in marrying a man half her age. Her choice fell on an obscure young American, William Ashmead Bartlett. After the forthcoming marriage was announced in July 1880, Angela came under intense pressure to change her mind. She was not dissuaded, and rightly so, for Bartlett proved to be a devoted husband. They remained happily together for twenty-five years until Angela's death at the age of 92 in 1906. She was buried in Westminster Abbey at the foot of the memorial to Lord Shaftesbury, her friend and fellow benefactor of the poor.

At its peak in the 1890s, Strand was known as London's High Street. The hordes of suburban shoppers who poured into Charing Cross station made a beeline for the Civil Service store where they could buy everything from a flower vase to curtain material to a packet of pins. The store had its origins in the Civil Service Supply Association set up as a co-operative venture by a group of General Post Office clerks who realised they could buy goods at a discount by joint purchasing. The co-operative was so successful, it created its own premises first in Victoria Street and then, in 1877, as busi-ness continued to expand, at 425 Strand where it developed into a fully-fledged department store. With its most improbable name as a marketing brand, the Civil Service store, rebuilt in Art Deco style, continued as a business until 1982 when it closed after a calamitous fire. What we see now is a nondescript block of offices and flats with the stationer Ryman occupying the corner site.

At 399 Strand is Stanley Gibbons, a reminder of my young days when almost every boy though, not as I recall, many girls, was an avid stamp collector. Starting in 1856, Edward Stanley Gibbons, then aged sixteen, turned his passion for stamps into a profitable business. The company gained worldwide status with the Stanley Gibbons catalogue, an essential guide for philatelists. With the decline of stamp collecting as a popular hobby, Stanley Gibbons has survived frequent changes of ownership and a period of insolvency in 2022 when the company took out a £6.5 million loan to buy the British Guiana 1c magenta, the world's rarest stamp.

Of all Strand retailers now long gone, the hardest to credit is the Wenham Lake Ice Company which thrived in the days before refrigeration. Sold in blocks to householders and restaurants, the ice was imported from Wenham Lake, north east of Boston and close to the shortest sea route across the Atlantic. Half the cargo melted *en route* but there was enough left over to make for a profitable business. To promote its wares, the Wenham Lake shop displayed in its window a large block of ice behind which the front page of a newspaper could be read through the ice. Passers-by were suitably enthralled.

Several shops sold mineral water touted as miracle cure for sundry illnesses. One of the earliest vendors was Daniel Gach whose premises were in Craven Street connecting Strand to

Northumberland Avenue. The water sold by Gach came from the East Ashton Mineral Well near Trowbridge in Wiltshire. Not given to understatement, Gach asserted that:

By drinking and washing with the Water, more than 100 persons have been already cured of Wounds, from one to upwards of twenty years standing, of Scorbutical Eruption, of sore Eyes, sore Breasts, the Leprosy and the King's Evil.

All comers in search of enlightenment on topics such as the abolition of slavery were welcomed to the public meetings at Exeter Hall on the site of what is now the Strand Palace Hotel. Opened in 1831, Exeter Hall was London's largest public venue where the main auditorium could seat 4,000, while a second auditorium accommodated up to a thousand. For such a large space the façade was uncharacteristically modest with a recessed entrance behind two Corinthian columns. This at least allowed for control over the numbers trying to get in but presented problems when audiences were scrambling for the exit onto a Strand crowded with horse-drawn vehicles.

There was also a problem with the acoustics. Cheers or groans in the big auditorium could be heard throughout the building, interrupting meetings in the smaller venues. In the absence of artificial aids, chairing a meeting could be hard while chairing a rowdy meeting was all but impossible.

Events at Exeter Hall ranged from a seven-hour public meeting in 1834 to support a free colony of South Australia to campaigns for overseas missions of various Christian sects. The Hall was also used for concerts. Hector Berlioz conducted here in 1852 and 1855.

One who could generate a full house at Exeter Hall was the bible-thumping preacher, Charles Haddon Spurgeon who preached here on nineteen occasions. Spurgeon's pulling power was as much a tribute to his entertainment value as to his sharing eternal truths. At a time when there were few rival attractions, a preacher who could play on the emotions of his congregation was the equal of a great actor. Short and round, Spurgeon was no matinee idol. 'He has high shoulders and low forehead and none of the beauty of holiness; his voice is not harmonious and his appearance ungraceful.' But what Spurgeon lacked in physical presence was more than compensated by strength of personality and oratorical skills. With his phenomenal memory (he claimed to be able to identify by name up to five thousand of his followers) he had a talent for convincing whoever he met that they were somehow unique in his eyes.

He spoke a language ordinary people could understand. In keeping his message simple he gave an interpretation of the Bible which left no room for doubt. The Bible was divinely inspired; the essence of faith was trust. This could get dangerously close to tautology; to believe, you had to believe. 'Those who do not believe are like the condemned man in his cell. He that believeth not is condemned already'. His emotional power was soul-stirring. As an eye-witness recorded, 'While he was preaching, I felt as if I was the only one in that great audience he was speaking to ... I was never so touched by a sermon in my life ... In fact, I could not restrain my tears, so exactly did he specify me'.

Spurgeon caught on to the Victorian love of melodrama. On facing death: 'It may come to us on a sudden ... What think ye? What think ye? Could you gather up your feet in the bed and look into eternity without feeling the cold sweat of fear stand upon your brow?' As he spoke he roamed the platform, pausing often to direct comments at someone who had caught his attention. He had no need for notes and though he must have prepared what to say, at least in outline, his sermons had to be recorded in shorthand. When published they sold in millions.

Spurgeon's base was the Metropolitan Tabernacle at the Elephant and Castle. Miraculously, this tribute to Victorian religious enthusiasm has survived in a district that has suffered more than its share of demolition and brutalist rebuilding. Less fortunate was the Exeter Hall. Eventually taken over by the Young Men's Christian Association (YMCA) it was sold to Joe Lyons group of restaurants and hotels in 1907 and immediately demolished.

Before the Royal Courts of Justice were built at the Aldwych end of Strand, Craven Street was popular with lawyers for its proximity to Westminster Hall where all the major cases were heard. The legal reputation was parodied in popular verse

In Craven Street, Strand, ten attorneys find place,
And ten dark coal-barges are moored at its base;
Fly, Honesty, fly! Seek some safer retreat,
For there's craft in the river, and craft in the street.

Benjamin Franklin, scientist, diplomat and a founding father of the United States lived at 36 Craven Street from 1757 to 1774. His home is now a museum aptly known as Benjamin Franklin House. Other illustrious names associated with Craven Street include the German poet Heinrich Heine at No. 32 and Herman Melville (*Moby Dick*) who lodged at No. 25 in 1849 when, as a sailor, he visited London.

Where Strand joins Fleet Street, Temple Bar marked the dividing line between the City of London and the City of Westminster, the two power centres of the medieval English monarchs. The name derives from the Temple Church, while the Temple, once the heartbeat of the Knights Templar has long been home to the Inns of Court where many of London's leading barristers reside. An ancient ceremonial has the monarch halting at Temple Bar where the Lord Mayor hands over the Sword of State as a token of loyalty.

Temple Bar has had many incarnations. While the old wooden version survived the Great Fire of 1666, it was rebuilt in Portland stone under the direction of Sir Christopher Wren as part of the general redevelopment of the City. This two-storey structure, the wide central arch flanked by two narrower arches, outlasted all the other principal gateways to the City of London (Ludgate, Newgate, Aldersgate, Cripplegate, Moorgate, Bishopsgate and Aldgate) but with an ever-increasing traffic flow its charm was sacrificed to commerce.

In 1878, as part of road widening, Temple Bar was dismantled, the stone put into storage. Two years later, the wealthy brewer,

Henry Meux, bought the remains and had them re-erected as a gatehouse for his estate in Hertfordshire. There it remained until 2004 when again it was dismantled and returned to the City of London for reconstruction as the entrance to Paternoster Square close to St Paul's Cathedral. A memorial to mark the site of the original Temple Bar stands in front of the Royal Courts of Justice, the last great secular building of the Victorian Gothic revival.

The Gothic style was the product of the Victorian love affair with medievalism, the fashionable escape 'from the frightening implications of the present and future into the romantic past' (John Steegman, *Victorian Taste*). The leading role in promoting Gothic was taken by the established Church of England, a powerhouse in Victorian Britain, which associated Gothic with piety and learning, a contrast to modernism with its brutalisation of work and vulgarisation of leisure.

New Anglican churches of which there were over 2,500 in the half century up to 1876 were almost exclusively Gothic as too were the many old churches adapted to contemporary needs. Architects who specialised in Gothic such as George Gilbert Scott, whose masterpiece is the Grand Midland Hotel at St Pancras International, had their work cut out to keep up with the demand for their services. So it was that when Parliament decided it was time for a purpose-built structure to accommodate the various central courts, Gothic had the edge.

With its elevated view of its place in the affairs of man, the legal profession aspired to a hub that melded grandeur with dignity, the majesty of the law harmonising with the majesty of the

Church. The selection committee of eminent justices decided on a competition to find an architect best suited to their needs. Twelve architects submitted designs, almost all of them opting for a Gothic colossus with conspicuous ecclesiastical associations.

Finding it hard to agree on a single applicant, the committee came to the ludicrous decision to divide the work between Edward Barry, whose father had directed the rebuilding of the Houses of Parliament after the 1834 fire, and George Edmund Street, a deeply religious man who had started his career in the office of Gilbert Scott. There followed an acrimonious debate which ended, as might have been predicted, with the realisation that responsibility of the design had to fall on just one pair of shoulders. The consensus favoured Street.

There must have been time when Street regretted his prestigious commission. After a six-acre site was cleared of 450 houses, work started on a building that was beset with problems, not least a labour dispute which led to the employment of German stone masons who were not made to feel thoroughly welcome. That Gothic required intricately modelled elevations and interiors put more pressure on Street who prided himself on his eye for detail.

The Royal Courts were opened in 1882 by Queen Victoria. Street was not there to see the culmination of his work. He had died a year earlier of overwork and exhaustion.

Architectural critics have damned the Royal Courts with faint praise. Nikolaus Pevsner described the building as an 'object lesson in free competition' while David Brownlee sees it as a 'regular mongrel affair'. The debt to conventional church design is immediately apparent with the arched doorway leading to the Great Hall, a cathedral setting in all but name. The question then as now is whether the cause of justice might be better served by a secular building with more attention to a proficient administration of the law.

Close by on the other side of Strand is Twinings. The symbiotic relationship between Twinings and Britain's favourite non-alcoholic beverage has its origins in London's first tea room at 216 Strand. It opened in 1706 and is still there today. The firm's distinctive entrance, created in 1787, features two Chinese figures representing the origins of tea in China.

From a family of Gloucestershire weavers, Thomas Twining was an entrepreneurial genius who was first to recognise the potential of tea as a rival drink to coffee. To back his judgement he bought Tom's Coffee House on Strand where tea found increasing favour. With the fashion among wealthy families for tea to be served at afternoon gatherings of high society ladies, Thomas Twining provided dry tea of various blends.

While Thomas was succeeded by his son Daniel, the business expanded to include exports to America though there is no foundation in the rumour that it was Twinings tea that was tossed into the sea at the famous Boston Tea Party.

Across the way from the Royal Courts on its own little island is St Clement Danes Church. Of medieval origin, St Clement Danes was rebuilt by Sir Christopher Wren and rebuilt again after it was gutted in the Blitz. Legend has it that the church might, just might, have inspired the nursery rhyme *Oranges and Lemons*.

Be that as it may, the bells of St Clement's play the tune of *Oranges and Lemons* daily at 9.00am, noon, 3.00pm and 6.00pm. As from 1958, St Clement Danes became the Central Church of the Royal Air Force holding Books of Remembrance to all who died in service.

Outside the church is the statute of Marshal of the Air Force, Arthur Harris, a controversial war leader who, in 1944, ordered the firebombing of Dresden, causing the death of 25,000 civilians. It was a 'truly horrifying event' says Harris's biographer Henry Probert but whether the attack on a cultural landmark and mass civilian deaths was justified by the exigencies of total war remains a cause of historical dispute.

On a more peaceful note, on the Fleet Street side of St Clement Danes is a statue of Dr Johnson whose seminal diction-ary was completed in 1755. His own definition of a lexicographer was 'a harmless drudge'. The dedication on Johnson's statue de-clares him to have been a 'Critic, Essayist, Philologist, Biographer, Wit, Poet, Moralist, Dramatist, Political Writer and Talker'. Quite a lot to pack into one lifetime.

No account of Strand would be complete without a mention of the BBC which had its first home in Savoy Place. It was es-tablished under royal charter in 1922 as the British Broadcasting Company with a brief to 'inform, educate and entertain'. This it attempted to do with minimal resources for ten years before what is now the British Broadcasting Corporation moved to the pur-pose-built Broadcasting House on Portland Place.

As the first head of drama, Val Gielgud recalled that the quality of radio output was largely determined by creating convincing sound effects. For his part, 'it was entertaining to watch potatoes being rolled on a drum to simulate an avalanche; a matchbox being crumpled to represent a splintered iceberg and the combined operation of a bath and roller skate to bring a train into or out of a country station'.

In October 1931, Jack Payne and his band made history by broadcasting before television cameras at Savoy Hill, the first televised programme put out by the BBC.

The title of the chapter is from a music hall song: 'Let's all go down the Strand, have a banana!' Why have a banana? Please don't ask.

10

Rules, the oldest restaurant in Covent Garden

A Good Night Out

Cookshops; Chop houses; Early restaurants: Rules, Simpsons-in-the-Strand, Romanos; Richard D'Oyly Carte; Gilbert and Sullivan; George Grossmith and the Savoy Operas; Opening of the Savoy Hotel.

The first mention of something approaching a conventional restaurant in Covent Garden appears in the diary of Samuel Pepys. In May 1667, he took his wife out for dinner and:

> *Bethought our selves to go to a French house...and so enquired out Monsieur Robins, my periwig-maker who keeps an ordinary, and in an ugly street in Covent Garden did find him at the door, and so we went in; and in a moment almost had the table covered, and clean glasses, and all in the French manner, and a mess of potage first, and then a piece of boeuf-à-la-mode, all exceedingly well seasoned and to our great liking; at least it would have been anywhere else but in this bad street, and in a periwig-maker's house; but to see the pleasant and ready attendance that we had, and all things so desirous to please, and ingenious in the people, did take me mightily. Our dinner cost us 6s.*

This was a considerable outlay at a time when there were taverns that offered a substantial meal at half the price. Later, Pepys wrote of his experience at Chatelin's, the French house in Covent Garden 'and there had a dinner that cost us 8s. 6d. apiece, a base dinner, which did not please us at all'.

A more satisfactory evening was to be had at the Half-Moon Tavern at the junction of Half-Moon Alley and Strand. It was managed by Jean le Becq, a French Huguenot famed for his kitchen. The tavern retained its reputation for good cooking after le Becq's death about 1730 when it was renamed The Key after the new proprietor, Thomas Key.

By the end of the seventeenth century cookshops served cuts of roast meat. The customer made his choice from one of several turning spits. From Jonathan Conlin's closely-researched study of London and Paris (*Tales of Two Cities*) we learn that standards of the cookshops were not of the best. Their cheap fare appealed to coachmen, chairmen (those who carried sedan chairs) and footmen who supposedly didn't mind being served 'measly Pork, rusty Bacon, stinking Lamb, rotten Mutton, slinked Veal [that is from a prematurely-born calf], and Coddled Cow, with yellow Greens, sooty Pottage, and greasy Pudding. Cookshops were particularly common behind St-Martin-in-the-Fields, a neighbourhood known as Potage Island'.

The cookshops gave way to chop houses, commonly known as 'slap bang shops', a dubious tribute to the speed of service.

Food was eaten at simple tables of booths, with partitions or curtains to provide some separation between groups of diners, each place being supplied with a cruet of sauce and a hook for one's hat. Again the focus was on roast meat. Beans or salad could be ordered, as well as cheese and sweet tarts, but no fish, nothing with a sauce and no fiddly sweet dishes.

At supper houses such as Paddy Green's 'you could eat the succulent chop with well-baked potato, floury and squeezed from its jacket by the deft waiter'.

Under the Piazza was the Shakespeare's Head Tavern where, from 1736, John Twigg gained a reputation as a first class cook, his speciality being turtle soup. Twigg was a poor boy who had made good. Born and bred in the Garden, he recalled playing marbles in the alley between the Piazza and Hart Street (now Floral Street). A fixture at the Shakespeare's Head for over half a century, Twigg attracted the *haut ton* including 'the gentlemen educated at Eton School' who gathered regularly to enjoy exceptional cooking.

The oldest extant restaurant in Covent Garden is Rules in Maiden Lane. Originally an oyster bar when Thomas Rule opened for business in 1798, the menu soon extended to traditional English cuisine appealing to actors, writers and others of the bohemian set who delighted in turning a meal into a social occasion. Rules has had several makeovers and has long since severed its connection with the Rule family. But, it retains its links with the past as evidenced in the hundreds of prints and sketches that adorn the walls. The poet and conservationist, John Betjeman described the restaurant as a 'unique and irreplaceable part of literary and theatrical London'.

Another restaurant with a venerable culinary tradition, and happily still with us, is Simpson's-in-the-Strand. Starting life as a coffee house, it became something more in the 1850s as the place to go for roast meats served from dinner trolleys wheeled to the tables for guests to choose their cut. Bought by Richard D'Oyly Carte in 1898 to add to his Savoy portfolio, Simpson's entered its golden age when it came to represent old England at its finest. Lt. Col. Newnham-Davis, who holds the distinction of being

London's first restaurant critic, gave a fulsome account of his lunch at Simpson's where tradition and opulence melded perfectly.

The big dumbwaiter in the centre of the room, almost as tall as a catafalque, with its burden of glasses and decanters, and four plated wine-coolers, one at each corner of the ornament, the divisions with brass rails and little curtains that run down one side of the room; the horsehair stuffed, black-cushioned chairs and lounges, the mirrors on one side of the room and the ground-glass windows on the other; the painted garlands of flowers and fish and flesh and fowl, mellowed by age and London smoke, that fill up the vast spaces on the wall, the ormolu clocks, the decoratively folded napkins in glasses on the mantelpiece, the hats and coats hanging in the room, the screen with many time-tables on it, the great bar window opening into the room, framing a depth of luminous shadow, all are old-fashioned. Only the two great candelabra that stand, a dozen feet high, on either side of the room have been modernised.

The waiter, 'a rubicund gentleman of portly figure dressed in white', took the order which he then delivered to one of the carvers 'who duly arrived at the table with his trolley of delights'.

In the first of his Blandings novels, published in 1915, P.G. Wodehouse describes Simpson's as a 'restful Temple of Food'.

Its keynote is solid comfort. Country clergymen, visiting
London for the annual Clerical Congress, come here to
get the one square meal which will last them till next
year's Clerical Congress. Fathers and uncles, with sons
or nephews on their hands rally to Simpson's with silent
blessings on the head of the genius who founded the place,
for here only can the young boa-constrictor really fill
himself at moderate expense. Militant suffragettes come
to it to make up leeway after their last hunger-strike.

Though loaded with tradition, in the early part of the last century, Rules and Simpson's were outclassed by the legendary Romano's, the popular haunt in Strand of:

...people of the theatre, of the Stock Exchange, the Bar,
journalists, playwrights, soldiers, sailors, painters,
black-and-white artists, explorers, planters and country
squires – as mixed a collection as ever congregated
habitually under one roof, but welded together in a
species of clannishness, resembling the membership of a
small and intimate club.

This tribute was from J.B. Booth a sports journalist who was a regular at Romano's in its great days.

Romano himself, otherwise known as Roman, was a character to beat all characters. A small swarthy man with thick black hair and, his pride and joy, a carefully tended waxed moustache, he was an Italian out of central casting. It was his very own version of his adopted language spoken rapidly, that enchanted his customers who could always be sure that Romano would stop by the table. 'Your lunch, evet'hing go alla right, eh, mister Esquire?' Many tales were told of Roman's uncertain grasp of English. A keen follower of the horses, he made an urgent enquiry of one of his customers who had lately returned from a Kempton Park meeting: 'Hi! You? Missa Shif! What win de Nateral Gland Bleeders Coal Stakes?'

Who can doubt that it was all part of the act? Quality was the first requirement. Roman boasted 'the best macaroni in London' and one of the best wine cellars. An inflexible rule at Romano's was that no bill could be questioned. Yet credit, scored up in chalk on slates, was always on offer to regular customers going through a bad patch. Inevitably Romano's entered into the Wodehouse collection of wild nights in high society. In *Pigs Have Wings*, Galahad Threepwood recalled seeing Major 'Plug' Basham, 'throw a side or beef at a fellow in Romano's, laid him out cold'.

The Great War was a turning point for Romano's, as for so many Edwardian institutions. It survived for many years but, said the theatre historian W. Macqueen-Pope, 'it was never quite the same, never quite so free and easy, never quite the same true piece of Bohemia'.

On the other side of Strand towards Trafalgar Square was the Hotel Cecil, much favoured by veterans of service in India. Not surprisingly, the Hotel Cecil was reported to serve the best curries in London. When restaurant critic Newnham-Davis called in one evening he found that the dish of the day was Ceylon curry – 'a tender spring-chicken for the foundation of the curry, and all the accessories, Bombay duck that crumpled in our fingers to dust, paprika cakes, thinner than a sheet of notepaper, and chutnees galore to add to the savoury mess'.

Newnham-Davis was well satisfied with his meal at £3 including wine and brandy.

The Hotel Cecil came down in 1930 to be replaced by Shell Mex House, an unlovely building which boasted the largest clock face in Europe, or so the pleasure boats would have it as they passed by on the Thames. A green plaque on the Strand entrance commemorates the foundation in 1918 of the Royal Air Force which had its first headquarters at Hotel Cecil.

Then, as now, the grandest place for eating and entertaining in Covent Garden and Strand is at the Savoy, a hotel, restaurant and theatre all in one. The Savoy has its origins in the collaboration of composer Arthur Sullivan and lyricist William S. Gilbert with the impresario Richard D'Oyly Carte. For those of us who have enjoyed the fruits, it was a partnership made in heaven though there were many occasions when the principals would have argued for the other place.

While Carte, a brilliant entrepreneur, was driven by an obsession to create the best whether it was a theatre, hotel or stage performances, the artistic side of the business had to contend with a spendthrift composer who valued his leisure, lots of it, and a cantankerous lyricist who was ever convinced that Carte was taking an unfair share of the profit from their creative talent. For his part, Carte felt unappreciated. Whatever the tensions, and after a shaky start, the second Gilbert and Sullivan operetta was a resounding success. A satire on the legal profession, *Trial by Jury*, set the tone with a pompous judge who tells how he rose from clerical drudgery to legal eminence.

When I, good friends, was called to the bar,
I'd an appetite fresh and hearty
But I was, as many young barristers are,
An impecunious party.

But he soon got the measure of the profession by falling in love with 'a rival attorney's elderly, ugly daughter'. His prospective father-in-law foresaw a bright future.

'You'll soon get used to her looks', he said,
And a very nice girl you'll find her
She may easily pass for forty three
In the dusk with the light behind her.

Political correctness was not part of Gilbert's makeup.

Well into its run the *Daily Telegraph* reported that the short operetta 'gets better than ever…The true enjoyment of laughter has not yet been discovered by those who have not seen *Trial by Jury.*'

Forty-five minutes long, *Trial by Jury* was followed by the more substantial *HMS Pinafore*, premiered in May 1878 at the Opera Comique in Wych Street just off Strand. The Opera Comique was said to be the worst designed theatre in London with its four entrances from four different streets. To reach the auditorium, audiences had to find their way along a series of tunnels. The theatre and street were demolished in 1902 as part of the development of Aldwych and Kingsway.

Pinafore hit the satirical bullseye with the caricature of Sir Joseph Porter, a self-serving incompetent who bears comparison to one or two of today's politicians.

> *I grew so rich that I was sent*
> *By a pocket borough into Parliament*
> *I always voted at my party's call.*
> *And I never thought of thinking for myself at all.*
> *I thought so little, they rewarded me*
> *By making me the Ruler of the Queen's Navee!*

Pinafore made a star of George Grossmith. He is known today as the co-author, with his brother Weedon, of *The Diary of a Nobody*, a satire on lower middle-class aspirations that revolved around the Pooters and their wayward son Lupin. Home for the Pooters was a Victorian villa ('a nice six-roomed residence, not counting basement') off the Holloway Road, still known locally as Pooterland.

When, in 1892, after appearing as a series of articles in *Punch*, the *Diary* was published as a book, Grossmith was already an established writer, composer and performer, a principal of the Savoy Operas and all-round entertainer, much in demand as a solo act for high society parties.

He had started his career in his father's footsteps as a court reporter. Drawing on his experiences of judicial proceedings for *Punch*, it was a short step to giving lectures and dramatic recitations. Charles Dickens had given the lead. The young Grossmith traded on the master's popularity by giving his own version of scenes from Dickensian life, together with improvisations from Mark Twain, George Eliot and Thomas Hood. It was not long before he was producing his own material. Small and dapper, he made up for dramatic shortcomings with a frenetic energy that delighted audiences. It helped that he was an accomplished pianist 'for whom,' said critic Percy Fitzgerald, 'his pianoforte was almost an instinctive form of expression like the human voice'. His speciality was the comic song. The catchiest of his tunes, *See Me Dance the Polka*, required a gymnastic display from Grossmith as he danced and worked the keys simultaneously.

In October 1877, the small and dapper Grossmith was surprised by an offer from Arthur Sullivan to play the leading role in *The Sorcerer*, his latest collaboration with W.S. Gilbert. Such was Grossmith's triumph in *The Sorcerer*, and despite looking not in the least like a traditional opera star, he became the first choice to top the bill in *HMS Pinafore*, *The Pirates of Penzance*, *Patience*, *Iolanthe* and *Princess Ida*.

Given Gilbert's acerbic nature, it comes as no surprise that Grossmith's relationship with the librettist could be edgy. For *Princess Ida*, Grossmith had just two lines in the first act.

King Gama (Grossmith): Must we, till then, in prison cell be thrust?

King Hildebrand: You must!

King Gama: This seems unnecessarily severe!

Having turned up at rehearsal time and again for this modest contribution, Grossmith lost patience. He moved to the footlights to address Sullivan in the stalls.

> *'Could you tell me, Sir Arthur, what the words "this seems unnecessarily severe" have reference to?'*

> *Sullivan replied: 'Because you are to be detained in prison, of course.'*

> *'Thank you,' said Grossmith, 'I thought they had reference to my having been detained here three hours a day for the past fortnight to sing them'.*

An open row broke out when Gilbert complained that Grossmith was overacting. A letter bluntly accusing him of gagging started an acrimonious exchange, with Grossmith taking offence at the suggestion that he was unprofessional. He wrote: 'I hold a position in my profession which is nearly equivalent to the one you hold in yours, and I expect to be treated with a certain amount of courtesy.' As to gagging, 'My occasional mild interpolations have been spontaneous, intermittent and seldom repeated', adding that he had never altered any of Gilbert's lines. Gilbert backtracked with a muted apology.

After 1889, Grossmith gave up on operetta to return to his solo show of song, dance and mimicry. Immaculate in evening dress with sleek brown hair, a carnation in his buttonhole, and a pince-nez firmly on his nose, he was a sell-out across Britain and

America. After performing at Balmoral, Queen Victoria complimented 'a very funny little man'.

As director, as well as lyricist, Gilbert was the master of the acerbic put down. Woe betide those who challenged his autocracy. The actor-manager Seymour Hicks recorded examples of Gilbert's style.

> *Having gone back and back in a part with a well-known actor until he was tired, [Gilbert] left the stage for the stalls and said: 'Now we'll begin all over again.' The actor, who no doubt was angry at being sent over the words so often and shown up before a large company, thought he would cross swords with Mr. Gilbert and save his face by picking a quarrel. He waited till he was told again it was all wrong; for about the hundredth time, and then, stepping down to the footlights, he shouted to the man of a thousand Savoy delights: 'Mr. Gilbert, I am not a very good-tempered man.' 'No,' said Gilbert, 'I'm not considered to have the temper of a saint either.' 'But I'd like you to understand, Mr. Gilbert, that I am a very strong man.' 'Really?' said Gilbert. 'Well, I stand six feet four in my stockinged feet, but if you want to know the difference between us I am an extremely clever man'.*

And again:

It was to a singularly imperfect actor at rehearsal ...
that Gilbert made a remark which has become a stock
rejoinder in the theatre. The victim called out: 'Look
here, Mr. Gilbert, I know my lines.' 'I know you do,'
rapped out Gilbert, 'but you don't know mine.'

D'Oyly Carte's dream project to build a theatre specifically for English light opera, began to take shape after he acquired land reclaimed from the river. Opening in 1881, the original frontage overlooked the Thames. Next to the theatre was a patch of waste land on which Carte put up a shed to house an electric generator, the power created by steam engines. The first public building to be entirely illuminated by electricity, the Savoy's auditorium was cool and airy with comfortable seating and clear sightlines. Handed free programmes, attractively produced, audiences were shown to their seats by attendants who broke with tradition by not expecting to be tipped. With the premieres of Gilbert and Sullivan's *Patience*, the Savoy was a triumph, thriving on a succession of classic operettas.

Gilbert and Sullivan's relationship with each other and with their producer was never easy. While the cantankerous Gilbert enjoyed nothing better than taking it out on social pretentions, the relatively easy-going Sullivan, who hated conflict and loved to be loved, was only too happy to embrace the social elite. It is no coincidence that Sullivan was first in line for a knighthood, awarded in 1883. Gilbert had to wait over twenty years for the same distinction. The partnership broke up and the relationship with D'Oyly Carte ended with a silly dispute over sharing the cost of a carpet bought for the Savoy theatre.

Carte meanwhile was devoting his energies to occupying the land next to his theatre by building a luxury hotel with electric light throughout, 'ascending rooms' or lifts, private bathrooms and running hot water, a break with the custom of providing guests with hot water only on request.

After a slow start, Carte sought a management team that would raise the stock of the Savoy to unprecedented heights. He found what he was looking for by headhunting César Ritz who had already acquired a reputation in France and Germany for superior dining in elegant surroundings. With Ritz came Auguste Escoffier, one of the greatest chefs of his generation. They were soon to be joined by an inspired maître d'hôtel known simply as Joseph. Born in Birmingham of French parents, Joseph made cookery an all absorbing passion of his life. 'If I had the choice', he declared, 'between going to the theatre to see Coquelin and Madam Bernhardt, and watching the faces of six true gourmets eating the perfect dinner, I should choose the latter'.

A distinctive personality with bushy eyebrows, tiny moustache, a bald crown to his head but with long and curly hair, Joseph brought the all-important personal touch to the culinary art, one who made it a mission to acknowledge all the regular diners, welcoming them by name.

The Ritz collaboration with Carte lasted for seven highly profitable years with Carte making more money from his hotel than from his theatrical enterprises which included highly successful Gilbert and Sullivan American tours. Wildly extravagant dinners were a hallmark of the Savoy. On a memorable evening, the courtyard was flooded and Caruso sang to the guests from a gondola in an imitation Venetian canal. Then there was a Japanese dinner served in a Japanese garden. Another dinner which achieved fame was given by a financial magnate to celebrate a colossal win at Monte Carlo, the decorations being black and red, even the waiters wearing red shirts and red gloves, and the lucky number on which the fortune had been won appearing everywhere in various forms. A white and green dinner, had fruit-trees bearing fruit, growing apparently through the tables with each chair a bower of foliage.

Carte and Ritz, both egotistical and strong-willed, were bound to fall out. The break came with the misplacement – Carte called it a misappropriation – of a quantity of wine and spirits. Carte also claimed to have evidence of kickbacks from suppliers though it is hard to imagine that he was shocked at an almost universal practice in the hotel and restaurant trade. Handed his dismissal notice, Ritz contemplated legal action but was dissuaded by Escoffier. Instead, they decamped to Paris where the Ritz Hotel set the standard for excellence that was soon to be matched by the Ritz in London's Piccadilly.

However, the Savoy continued to prosper. In 1924, Arnold Bennett, whose novel *Imperial Palace*, was based on the Savoy, was given a guided tour. His observations were noted in his diary for February 2nd, where he marvelled at the efficiency of the staff:

Tale of the head of the cloak-room; had been there for ages; remembers people's faces, often without troubling as to their names. He took an overcoat from an old gentleman, and gave it back to him at the end without a word.

Guest: How did you know that this is mine?

Employee: I don't know, sir.

Guest: Then why did you give it to me?

Employee: Because you gave it to me, sir.

After Richard D'Oyly Carte died in 1901, his son Rupert, who took over as chairman, embarked on the modernisation of the hotel and theatre along with other properties in the group, such as Claridge's. The expansion of the Savoy in 1903-4 included moving the main entrance for the hotel and theatre from the embankment to Strand. The theatre had another refurbishment in 1929 when the interior was swept away to be succeeded by a striking art deco design.

To add lustre to the hotel, famous personalities were encouraged by favourable rates to set up home at the Savoy. As Olivia Williams tells us in her delightful and highly readable *Secret Life of the Savoy*:

Sarah Bernhardt moved with her red setter, Tosco; Lillie Langtry started her mornings there with an 11am flute of champagne; and Harry Selfridge made it his base when he arrived from Chicago, ready to open a London department store. Sir Thomas Dewar, the Scottish whisky heir, moved in and stayed for forty years. He wondered if he might be the longest-serving Savoy resident since John of Gaunt. American producer Charles Frohman lived there whenever he was in town for work. It was ideally placed for him, just across the road from Theatreland, and he ate every day at the Grill. As became tradition, on the day a resident's death was announced, their table would be left empty. When Frohman died in the sinking of the Lusitania during the First World War, not only was his table left empty but his friends paid for a plaque beside it.

After its latest refurbishment, the Savoy is entering a new chapter in the story of a luxury hotel.

As for Gilbert and Sullivan, while their comic operas remained popular with amateur operatic groups, main stream productions suffered from tired old routines, the copyright holders refusing to countenance any updating; even the costumes remained the same over the decades. It was only when the copyright ran out that a new generation of producers and directors gave a welcome boost to an operatic tradition that had more than passing relevance to modern audiences.

11

Interior of the Gaiety Theatre, London, 1869

A Song and a Chorus

Gatti Brothers; The Adelphi and Vaudeville theatres;
The Gaiety theatre; Gertie Millar; Showgirls marrying
into the aristocracy.

The story of the Gatti brothers, Carlo and Giovanni, became an inspiration to immigrant families settling in London. After starting out by selling ice cream and chocolates, they got together with another recent immigrant, Giuseppe Monico, to buy up none too salubrious properties close to Hungerford Market. The gamble was on the South Eastern Railway succeeding in its objective to extend its reach to Charing Cross. Once government permission was granted, those with property rights in the immediate area were sitting on a gold mine.

Having secured their financial base, the Gatti brothers branched out into restaurants and music halls. Gatti's Charing Cross Music Hall, adopting what was now a familiar programme of solo acts as a theatrical setting, found a home in Villiers Street under the arches of Charing Cross Station. Baroness Orczy, creator of *The Scarlet Pimpernel*, spent an evening at what she called the Old Arches, one of several names under which the Gatti brothers promoted their entertainment.

> *There was no stage, only a platform in the centre of the hall, where sat enthroned the manager at a rostrum when he announced the programme together with the name of the artiste about to perform and tapped the desk before him with a wooden hammer. The audience sat on seats and benches all-round the central platform, very much as they do round a prize-ring. A few privileged members in the audience were permitted to sit on the platform with the manager, but this privilege*

entailed the obligation to pay for that gentleman's
drinks.

Having no pretensions to be a top rank venue, Gatti's was the place for aspiring performers to try out their acts. One such was the Levy Sisters, three chubby young ladies who sang and danced in costumes that showed off their legs to tantalising effect on the chiefly male audience. One of several 'sister' acts doing the rounds, the Levy trio went on to make their fortune in American vaudeville.

With the fading popularity of the music halls, Gatti's was converted into a cinema until the war when it was used as a fire station. It came back to life when it was taken over by the Players' Theatre, originally at 43 King Street, where in the 1930s, it revived Victorian style variety. With the South African actor Leonard Sachs as the instigator and presenter of music hall at its best, the successful formula of the Players' Theatre was adapted to television with the *Good Old Days* from Leeds City Varieties enjoying a thirty-year run up to 1983. The Players' Theatre closed in 2002 and is now a performance venue attached to Heaven, the centre of gay London night life.

Round the corner in Villiers Street and into Strand, nine-teenth-century music hall was presented on a rather grander scale. Built on the site of the Tivoli Beer Garden, the Tivoli Theatre of Varieties had a proper stage and comfortable seating with ticket prices to match although poor sight lines were slated until the venue was refurbished by leading theatre designer Frank Matcham towards the end of the century. This 'wonderful transformation', as the theatre journal *The Era*, described it, was home to the top names of music hall including George Robey, Little Tich, Dan Leno and Marie Lloyd. To earn a living and to build their careers, music hall artists often performed three or four times in an evening, dashing from one music hall to another. Fuelled by alcohol and lacking sleep, they invariably died young of overwork.

The boom years ended in 1914 when the theatre was closed for the widening of Strand, a project delayed until after the Great War. In the 1920s the Tivoli, like Gatti's, was resurrected as a cinema to showcase movies made by MGM, an arrangement that lasted until MGM opened the Empire Theatre on Leicester Square. The Tivoli remained in business showing foreign language movies that might otherwise have failed to secure a release. The Tivoli closed finally in 1957 to be replaced by a department store and later by New South Wales House. It is now a block of shops and offices.

To return to the Gatti family, not content with their music hall and with other profitable enterprises such as generating electricity for local businesses and wealthy households, they moved into legitimate theatre with the purchase of the Adelphi, opposite the Tivoli. Famous for its melodramas known as 'Adelphi Screamers', and for stage adaptations of Charles Dickens's novels, the Adelphi was in need of renovation. The Gattis decided to enlarge the theatre and to open a restaurant. They also bought the neighbouring Vaudeville. Both theatres thrived on the fashion for musical comedies, a few of which (*Mr Cinders* 1929, *Bless the Bride* 1947, and *Salad Days* 1954) enjoy the occasional revival.

At the stage door of the Adelphi is a memorial plaque that speaks to the hazards of the acting profession. It was here, in 1897, that William Terriss, a star of his day, was stabbed to death by a jealous colleague. There are unreliable, if well publicised, accounts of Terriss's ghost putting in the odd appearance.

If for more than half a century, Strand was the hub of light entertainment, at its centre was the Gaiety. Built in 1818 at the eastern end of Strand, close to what is now Aldwych, the Gaiety was the inspiration of John Hollingshead, known as 'Practical' John for his gift of getting things done. Hollingshead had a modest upbringing in Hoxton in London's East End where there was little in the way of formal education. But Hollingshead had an insatiable curiosity and was a quick learner. Free to wander, he acquired an encyclopaedic knowledge of street life. This he turned to good account by writing articles for one of the many publications springing up in the wake of cheap, steam-powered printing.

Both Dickens and Thackeray recognised his talent. He was one of the first contributors to the *Cornhill Magazine* in 1859. As editor, Thackeray was intrigued to know how Hollingshead had acquired his skill as a journalist. 'In the streets', said his protégé, 'from costermongers and skittle-yards'. Dickens was quick to take him on to the staff of *Household Words* and to encourage his love of the theatre. He was given passes to the latest productions and met leading actors. In 1863 he was made drama critic of the *Daily News* and even wrote a play for the light comedy actor J.L. Toole.

The more he learned about the theatre, the more he wanted to be directly involved.

The story as told by the journalist J.B. Booth (*London Town*) was of Hollingshead making a direct approach to Lionel Lawson, proprietor of the *Daily Telegraph* and instigator of the Gaiety.

> '*I hear you are going to build a theatre in the Strand. I want to take it on.* '
>
> '*Well, have you got any money?*' asked Lawson
>
> '*Two hundred pounds and no debts*' replied Hollingshead
>
> '*That's not much, is it?*'
>
> '*Not a great deal, but I suppose I can get more if I want it*'.
>
> '*You shall have the theatre*' said Lawson and they shook hands on the deal.

Hollingshead was as good as his word. In short measure, he formed a syndicate to put up the capital to buy the Gaiety lease.

The aim was to open on 21 December 1868. It was a tight schedule with the last of the builders picking up their tools only ten minutes before the audience began to file in. With a capacity for two thousand paying customers, every seat was taken.

The programme was a musical bag of treats. The curtain raiser was *The Two Harlequins*, a short operetta. This was followed by a comedy drama adapted like so many short plays from the French and finally a burlesque by no less that W.S. Gilbert who had already made his name as a humourist but had yet to join forces with Arthur Sullivan.

A popular feature that was to become a staple ingredient of Gaiety entertainments was the chorus of young ladies chosen for their well-endowed figures and pretty faces. Their acting talent was secondary. With a chiefly male audience, Hollingshead knew what he was about. As he confessed later in his career, 'I am a licensed dealer in legs and short skirts'.

The Gaiety stalls were the preserve of wealthy young men about town known as 'mashers' or 'stage-door Johnnies'. They wore tight trousers, carried crutch sticks and made the silver toothpick a fashion accessory – hence their nickname, the 'Crutch and Toothpick Brigade'

Building on the popularity of his stage shows, Hollingshead opened a Gaiety restaurant with 'English, French and German cuisine and the choicest wines of finest vintage'. Playgoers could book an early supper before making their way through their own entrance into the theatre. After curtain down business picked up with the stage-door Johnnies entertaining chorus girls.

Sophisticates derided the Gaiety. The aesthete, Graham Robertson whose oh, so elegant slim-line image by John Singer Sargent can be seen in the National Portrait Gallery, had this to say:

The Gaiety Burlesques were not achievements to be remembered with pride; puns stood for wit, jingling rhyme carried along dull dialogue, the productions were

upon the ordinary pantomime lines, and the costumes
quite particularly ugly.

There were compensations. Robertson lavished praise on Nellie Farren, the fourth generation of an acting family, whose sparkling personality gave life to what was otherwise a lacklustre stage routine. Nellie was the unrivalled Queen of the Gaiety. It may have had something to do with it that burlesque always had a woman playing the male leading role. It was as Principal Boy that Nellie Farren made her reputation and it was in that role that she showed off her legs 'slender and straight – with straight knees, like a boy's'. Maybe that is what appealed to the sexually ambivalent Graham Robertson.

A rare Gaiety venture that sank with all hands was a comic opera called *Thespis or The Gods Grown Old*. This inspired whimsical piece was the first collaboration between W. S. Gilbert and Arthur Sullivan. Though the melodies were infectious, even Nellie Farren could not save the show. But, when it came to picking winners, Hollingshead had a proud record, his range extending well beyond theatrical fripperies. He persuaded the Comédie Française to give a six week season in 1879 and a year later he staged London's first Ibsen play, *The Pillars of Society*. He was active too in politics, leading a campaign to prevent the infringement of copyright by American producers and challenging censorship by introducing the high-kicking Can Can to Gaiety audiences.

When eventually Hollingshead played himself out by sheer exhaustion, he handed over the Gaiety management to George Edwardes, a large florid man with a deceptively languid manner, who had started out with D'Oyly Carte as his box office manager at the Opera Comique. He did not have an easy start at the Gaiety. Burlesques, performed by actors who had seen better days, were no longer pulling in the crowds. After a few disappointing seasons, he injected new life into the Gaiety with a string of musical comedies which relied on a chorus that could sing, dance and, occasionally, act.

To the despair of the press critics who yearned for more substantial fare, Edwardes could point to the box office receipts as proof of his knowing what the public wanted. Under his direction, close attention was given to encouraging young women whose charms persuaded the men in the audience that, with the help of opera glasses, they were gazing at the most fabulous creatures on earth.

The young, idle rich were quick to take note of the attractions of marrying out of their class. The first of the Gaiety Company to capture the heart of an aristocrat was Kate Vaughan who had trained as a ballet dancer. She married Colonel the Hon. Frederick Wellesley, younger son of the Earl of Cowley. Kate's successors aimed higher. After Connie Gilchrist married the Earl of Orkney, the unfortunately named singer, Rosie Boote, became the Marchioness of Headfort. The arch snob, but prescient diarist, Henry 'Chips' Channon, had lunch with the Marchioness of Headfort, née Rosie Boote, in February 1949. 'Bad food', he reported, 'but she is the supreme example of an actress who married a great name and position and never regretted it.' The marriage was a success and Rosie was accepted into society.

On the death of her first husband, composer Lionel Monckton, Gertie Millar, unrivalled star of a succession of musical comedies, married the Earl of Dudley, a former Governor-General of Australia. Gertie stayed loyal to her origins. Meeting her late in life, diarist James Lees-Milne found 'the same candour, suppressed bitchiness, lack of society nonsense, gaiety, generosity – in fact the old music hall qualities'.

Stage and society alliances were not confined to the Gaiety. A popular singer at Evans's Supper Rooms, the exuberant Val Rhys, was carried off by millionaire brewer, Sir Henry Meux. As Lady Meux, Val became a dedicated Egyptologist, creating a museum of rare artefacts on the family estate. A keen racegoer, her stable of thoroughbreds included a Derby winner.

The Gaiety became the first call for gentlemen of means in pursuit of a glamorous wife. When yet another favourite was snatched from the chorus, George Edwardes lost patience:

> *It's ingratitude, sheer ingratitude! I've done everything*
> *for her – taught her to pick up her aitches, clean her*
> *fingernails, had her teeth looked to, her appendix*
> *removed, her hair dyed, dressed her from her underclothes*
> *to her boots, and now, when she looks like making good,*
> *she marries!*

The consolation for Edwardes was the growing appeal of the stage to upper class youths, male and female. Attracted by the allure of the footlights, they were the backbone of musical comedy which invariably spoofed the aristocracy. Soon after the accession of George V, so the story goes, two chorus boys were chatting together on the stage before the curtain went up: 'I wonder is dear old George in tonight?' said one of them. G.M. Salter, the stage manager, overheard them. Shocked by their impertinence, he said pompously, 'I must ask you to remember that when you have occasion to refer to Mr George Edwardes in this theatre, you must refer to him as *Mister* George Edwardes and in no other manner!' 'Oh, I was talking about the King, old boy', drawled the chorister.

As familiar to the love-sick fans as to ladies of the chorus, was Tierney, the Gaiety stage door keeper. For cash in hand this crusty old seaman was happy to set up an assignation. If it did not work out, he was hardly to blame; there were no refunds. So successful was Tierney with his side-line, he was able to invest in property, the rents from which kept him going into a comfortable old age.

Tierney's successor was Jimmy Jupp, an ex-sergeant major with a heavy moustache. He was under orders never to allow a man into the girls' dressing rooms. While gifts in kind, such as jewellery were permitted, no money was to be given to a Gaiety Girl. Presumably, as one who had got rich by keeping a tight control of the finances, Edwardes had no wish for one of his girls to incur envy by flaunting wealth. As for Jupp, the lavish tips that came his way were mostly lost at the races.

While there were those of the social elite who were scandalised by the influx into their ranks of stage luminaries, the more perceptive saw it as a blessing. Said leading London hostess, Lady Dorothy Nevill,

*Matrimonial alliances between the aristocracy and
the stage have become so frequent as now scarcely to
attract attention...Many an old family has gained fresh
vigour from an infusion of fresh blood, and some of
these alliances have been accompanied by considerable
romance.*

It was a sentiment endorsed by dramatist Arthur Wing Pinero.
'The musical comedy girls will be the salvation of the aristocracy.'

The end of the century looked also to be the end of the
Gaiety. The site was needed by the London County Council for
a widening of Strand and for a new road to be called Kingsway
leading into what was soon to be known as Aldwych. However,
the Gaiety was to be resurrected on the corner of the junction
of Strand and Aldwych. Opening in October 1903, the new
Gaiety was a splendid piece of Italian renaissance architecture
with an eye-catching dome topped by a golden figure of a girl
blowing a trumpet. But the call was muted. While a weak vessel
such as *The Troubadour* could stay afloat for 675 performances,
the melodies were predictable and depended on the actors to
outperform indifferent material. Folk legend has bolstered the
reputation of second-rate shows by spotlighting the undoubted
talents such as Gertie Millar. The Gaiety closed finally in 1939,
remaining derelict until 1957 when it fell to the wrecking ball.
The site was taken over as the headquarters of English Electric, a
manufacturing company which announced its presence with two
giant nude male statues depicting Power and Speed. The sculpture

was by Sir Charles Wheeler, the President of the Royal Academy. Unfortunately his work was the subject of ribald jokes thought to detract from the dignity of the commerce inside the building. Power and Speed were removed and put in storage until a new home was found for them at Eltham College, a private day school in south east London. Meanwhile, the English Electric building on Aldwych was demolished in 2005 to be replaced by a hotel designed by Foster + Partners.

12

The Market today

Ring in the New

The Market changes hands; Sir Thomas Beecham; Waldorf Hotel; Ben Travers and the Aldwych farces; The Blitz; The Covent Garden Market Authority; The Market moves; Campaign saves historic buildings.

The bond between the Bedford family and Covent Garden Market remained unbroken for over three hundred years, a tribute, if nothing else, to the staying power of the British aristocracy. By the 1860s the Bedford Estate was beginning to question if the financial return from the Market was worth the increasing trouble of running it. Efforts to ease the congestion caused by overcrowding were welcomed but they failed to take into account London's rising population and, in consequence, the increased demand for fresh produce.

In 1874, the Bedford Estate tried and failed to sell the entire Covent Garden to Metropolitan Board of Works, the body responsible for the overall planning of central London. The Board was criticised for not doing its job but, deficient though it was in many regards, it could hardly be blamed for shying away from a large capital outlay which would then require the taxpayer to invest further huge sums to make Covent Garden fit for purpose.

The Corporation of the City of London also turned a cold shoulder. While the Corporation had long experience of operating markets (the Billingsgate fish market, the Leadenhall market for poultry, game and eggs, the Metropolitan market for cattle, sheep and horses at Islington and the Spitalfields market for fruit and vegetables, all came within its jurisdiction), Covent Garden with its cocky and truculent street traders was a challenge thought to be best avoided.

The way was now open for private interests to make an offer for some twenty acres and twenty-six streets comprising the core of Covent Garden. The leading contender was Harry Mallaby-Deeley (later Sir Harry), a Tory Member of Parliament and property speculator whose plausible manner won him friends in high finance. Exuding confidence, Mallaby-Deeley encouraged press reports that his takeover of Covent Garden was all but done and dusted, adding that no great changes were anticipated in the management of the Market. The Bedford Estate was not so easily taken in. When it became clear that Mallaby-Deeley was a long way short of the money to finalise the transaction, the Estate lost patience, turning instead to a syndicate headed by Sir Joseph Beecham whose family made its fortune on the sale of laxative pills.

Despite sitting on great wealth, Beecham was an innocent in matters of high finance. His involvement in Covent Garden came about after he fell in with James White, Jimmy to his many highly placed friends, 'one of that group of financial wizards', said Beecham's son Thomas, 'who appeared and vanished like comets in the sky...during the period 1910-1930'. Beecham senior was persuaded to make a down payment on a £2 million deal to buy the entire Covent Garden estate. With White as the mastermind, the plan was for a syndicate to float a public company to manage and, in due time, to sell off the estate either in parcels or as a whole. Beecham was then to be paid back the deposit with interest plus a bonus for his services as the financial backer. What could go wrong?

The answer was just about everything. With the outbreak of the Great War, the Treasury imposed a ban on the transfer of capital other than for war purposes. This left Beecham, aged 70 and in frail health, with a contract to buy a large property he did not want and could not afford without selling family assets at a time when the economy was at its lowest ebb.

Full of optimism, Jimmy White promised to come up with a plan of escape but when this failed to materialise, Beecham turned to his son Thomas who, up to then, had been preoccupied with his musical ambitions that were to lift him to the dizzy heights of Sir Thomas Beecham, one of the greatest orchestral conductors. Meanwhile, the Bedford Estate stuck to the contract that required a further payment from Beecham, increasing his exposure by a half million.

In 1917, Joseph Beecham's heart gave out leaving Thomas and his brother to sort out the mess. The deficiencies of Jimmy White as a financial adviser became painfully obvious. Promises were cheap and White handed them out like confetti, while from his offices in Strand he entertained lavishly at local hostelries. As Thomas put it with commendable restraint:

*'He (White) was dashing and effective in the opening
stages of a financial adventure but, later on, and
especially if there were occasion to make a wise retreat,
he was apt to become apprehensive, sometimes to the
point of panic.*

Hiring reputable accountants to negotiate with the Bedford
Estate, an agreement was signed in 1918 whereby in return for
the additional funding from Beecham, a Covent Garden Estate
Company was granted a mortgage for the outstanding sum ow-
ing. As for Jimmy White, having spent a fortune on race horses,
by 1927 he was facing insolvency, a prospect that led him to take
poison. He left his family penniless.

Sir Thomas Beecham's connection with Covent Garden
went beyond the financial management of the Market. During
the Great War, he devoted his musical talent to the Royal Opera
House while post-war, the Beecham Opera Company gave seasons of international opera that set new standards of excellence.
But by 1920, his resources were stretched to breaking point and
the Beecham Opera Company went into liquidation. His knighthood, awarded in 1916, was poor compensation for the failure
of a bold venture, embracing 120 operas in all, 60 of them were
either new to Britain or revivals after many years of neglect. Sir
Thomas returned to the Opera House podium and to the management of the theatre in 1933, remaining in command for six years.

The Royal Opera House had to wait until the 1990s for a
total refurbishment. At the cost of £10 million, the façade, foyer

and the auditorium, all dating from 1858, were incorporated into the new theatre which now has the magnificent Floral Hall as an integral part of the structure.

With its entrance on the Piazza is the London Transport Museum housed in what was originally part of the Market. A rich collection of exhibits reveal how London's public transport took shape from the horse-drawn omnibus to the world's first underground railway which in its early days, the 1860s, relied on steam locomotives. Trams and trolleybuses, powered by overhead wires, have long since retreated into history but the familiar double-decker red bus has also undergone many design changes since it first appeared in 1905.

The Great War intervening, ownership of Covent Garden did not change hands finally until 1918. Meanwhile, the directly-elected London County Council having succeeded the Metropolitan Board of Works, came up with four possible solutions to the problem of congestion in and around Covent Garden. The first, that it should be split into three or four smaller markets, looked good on paper but left open the delicate question of where those markets would be sited. Acknowledging the impracticalities, the other ideas involved moving the entire Market either to somewhere in the area of the London docks, then one of Europe's busiest trading hubs, or to St Pancras which had the virtue of available space, or to the area around County Hall, the newly built headquarters of the LCC on the Thames south bank. The Beecham syndicate was willing to sell but not at a knock-down price that would have made the deal attractive to the LCC.

In 1921, the government was persuaded by the LCC to set up a committee to consider the future of all of London's central markets. This led to a damning report on Covent Garden where buildings were said to be obsolete, inconvenient and badly lighted. Moreover, the Market was too far away from a railway terminus and the port of London. The poor suffered because there was no cheap shopping centre in the vicinity. Finally, 'the passage of horse and motor vehicles conveying the millions of tons of produce which are dealt with annually at the market thought the narrow streets of Central London adds greatly to the unnecessary traffic congestion. The highly perishable nature of some of the fruit dealt in at the Garden results in frequent economic loss through delay in transit.'

The Committee recommended 'in the strongest possible terms, that this market, the largest of its kind in the Kingdom, should be placed under a public authority with a view to its development in the interests of the trade and the consumer'.

As usually is the way with government committees of inquiry, the report was shelved while other, apparently more pressing matters, occupied the government of the day. A proposal the Market should be relocated to the fifty-six acre site of the former Foundling Hospital in Bloomsbury, was rejected by the LCC whose left-leaning majority on the Council was liable to give short shrift to capitalists of whatever stripe.

With hindsight, the LCC's intransigence did have one advantage. It protected the essential structure of Covent Garden that today gives pleasure to millions. What might have been is suggested by the creation of Kingsway and Aldwych at the start of the last century. Hundreds of properties (admittedly in poor condition) were swept away to make way for what was touted as a masterstroke of urban planning. Unique to London was an underground tramway from the Thames embankment, emerging close to Holborn station. When, sadly, the trams were succeeded by double decker buses, the underpass closed. In 1964, it was reconstituted, at least in part, as a one-way tunnel for ordinary traffic.

While Kingsway, itself a broad thoroughfare, satisfied the planners' dream for neat symmetry, it failed to match the appeal of the Parisian boulevards it was supposed to emulate. The office block architecture was uniformly dull. Aldwych is not much better. Designed in the days of imperial grandeur, Australia House and India House are imposing by nature of their size but otherwise of no great distinction while the kindest thing to say about Bush House is that it is best viewed from a distance. Built between 1925 and 1935 as a trade centre by American industrialist Irving T. Bush, Bush House was for many years the headquarters of the BBC World Service and is now part of Strand campus of King's College.

To continue the catalogue of misguided intentions, the 1817 Waterloo Bridge designed by John Rennie and said by John Betjeman to be 'the best bridge in London' was sacrificed to the increased traffic flow resulting from the rebuilding of the old London Bridge and the construction of the Victoria Embankment. Despite the assurance of engineers that the piers could be underpinned and a recommendation from a Royal Commission that Rennie's bridge should be saved, the LCC pressed ahead with plans for a much wider replacement. Ironically, the hideously ugly Hungerford foot bridge, deemed unsafe after dark, was allowed to survive until its Golden Jubilee successor was opened in 2002.

Back on Aldwych, the Waldorf Hotel, now the Waldorf Hilton, opened in 1908 to provide visitors with services that matched the top American hotels. The name is a tribute to William Waldorf Astor who contributed part of the initial investment. A popular feature of the hotel was the Palm Court where the tango was introduced as the latest dance craze. The Waldorf was one of the select group of hotels that boasted their own in-house band. Led by Howard Godfrey, the Waldorfians played daily at the Palm Court. The resident singer was the crooner Al Bowley whose popularity shot up when his best known numbers *Love is the Sweetest Thing* and *Goodnight Sweetheart* were recorded on 78rpm discs. Though his career was cut short by a German bomb, his voice on record still holds its seductive charm.

Other musical talents were nurtured by the Waldorf. When early in the century, Thomas Beecham was recruiting for a new orchestra, he happened to be dining at the Waldorf when the band featured a young violinist of exceptional ability. 'Following my request for a solo he complied with the finale of the Mendelssohn Violin Concerto taken at a speed which made me hold my breath'. This was Albert Simmons, 'the best English fiddler of his generation' who became principal violin in Beecham's orchestra.

The Waldorf is flanked on each side by a theatre. Opening in the same year as the hotel, the Strand, now the Novello, was built in grand Edwardian style with a plushly decorated auditorium. The change of name was a tribute to Ivor Novello, actor, dramatist and composer who lived above the theatre for 38 years. The Novello's twin theatre, the Aldwych, was the home to the World Theatre Seasons presented by Peter Daubeny from 1964 to his death in 1975 and was subsequently occupied by the Royal Shakespeare Company as their London base for twenty years. The prime niche for the Aldwych in theatrical history is reserved for the Aldwych farces which filled the theatre from 1922 to 1933. All but three of the twelve farces were written by Ben Travers, an unassuming man who was gifted with a sharp but never cruel wit. His break came with *A Cuckoo in the Nest* presented by actor-manager Tom Walls, which ran for a year at the Aldwych.

As the star of the show, Tom Walls played the archetypal randy middle-aged philanderer whose raised eyebrows conveyed an assortment of double meanings. His co-star was the monocled Ralph Lynn in the silly ass role and Robertson Hare, a short, bald put-upon character whose cry of woe, 'Oh, Calamity' accompanied the loss of some vital item of clothing, invariably his trousers, in embarrassing circumstances. The sex appeal was provided by Winifred Shotter who delighted audiences and shocked prudes by making her first appearance dashing across the stage clad in pink pyjamas.

As the guiding force of the Aldwych farces, Tom Walls was notoriously unreliable. Easily diverted by his love of horses (his April the Fifth won the 1932 Derby), he was casual in learning his lines. First night audiences at the Aldwych came to anticipate Walls turning to the wings to shout for a prompt. It was done with such style as to guarantee a round of applause. Most of the Aldwych farces were turned into movies with Ben Travers as scriptwriter. He remained very much in the background allowing the regular cast to take the credit.

Travers was favoured by longevity. He really came into his own with what he called his 'rediscovery' when he was well into his eighties. At age eighty-nine he had a new play, *The Bed Before Yesterday*, produced at the Lyric Theatre with Lindsay Anderson as director and Joan Plowright in the lead. Revivals of his earlier plays climaxed with the National Theatre production of *Plunder* in 1978.

Anecdotage was Travers's life blood. He appeared frequently on television chat shows where he could recreate the great days of the Aldwych farces with his fund of stories about Tom Walls, the commanding voice in every production. When Ben Travers died in December 1980 he was into his ninety-fifth year.

World War II brought to Covent Garden its share of death and disruption. At the height of the Blitz, Neal Street and Shelton Street took direct hits while in Maiden Lane, a delayed action bomb penetrated several floors of the Corps of Commissioners, those formidable gentlemen, nearly all ex-army, who stood outside hotels and restaurants to open doors or summon taxis. When the bomb exploded it sent up a shower of what looked like gold coins but was in fact a store of brass buttons that adorned commissioners' uniforms.

In 1941, a large fruit warehouse was destroyed in Bow Street. The bomb went through five storeys and exploded below the shelter. In *Westminster in War*, William Sansom describes

...the wooden-blocked market street littered with bricks and vegetables and straw, the great iron and glass dome of Covent Garden reflecting on its remaining glass that bright firelight, the lion-coloured palladium columns of the Opera deeply shadowed, and the spluttering roar of fire engines, the snakes of dead-grey hose winding through the mud and water flooding the street, the stolid façade of Bow Street Police Station, the fire spreading all around.

But most living of all in this street of nightmare were the unseen bodies entombed somewhere in the terrible breathing mound of debris. That was a powerless night for those standing, trying failing. The odds were too great. But mercifully, when days later the last of twenty bodies were recovered, it was found that each one had died instantly with the bomb's explosion.

The blackout was the chief disability suffered by the Market traders who, in the early hours, had to unload trucks in the pitch dark.

Even after peace was declared, fire was a constant hazard. In December 1949 the flames devastated the Christmas trees and other produce in the Flower Market. It burned for two days. One fireman died of suffocation and over forty others were treated at Charing Cross Hospital. Another fire, this in 1954 at a warehouse in Shelton Street, claimed three lives. It turned out that the place had been made a death trap by an insecticide that gave off an inflammable vapour.

Covent Garden theatres suffered during the war but the damage was inflicted largely by myopic politicians. In September 1939, all theatres, cinemas and other places of entertainment were told to close, thus marking one of the stupidest decisions in bureaucratic history. This order was soon rescinded but not before many West End shows had put up notices. The Royal Opera House became a dance hall while the Theatre Royal Drury Lane was adopted as the headquarters of the Entertainment National Service Association. ENSA was led by Basil Dean, a producer whose arrogance and autocratic manner did not go down well with popular performers who were accustomed to be treated with greater respect. Nevertheless, Dean succeeded in putting together an organisation that mounted shows wherever troops were based, at home or abroad. Most of the acting profession appeared under the ENSA banner at some point in the war, though not always with success. The comedian Tommy Trinder dubbed ENSA as Each Night Something Awful.

The problem was in meeting the demand for talent. It seemed that every amateur in the country – good, bad and frightful – was keen to offer their services. Auditions at Drury Lane were brisk to the point of cruelty. The dreaded shout from the stalls, 'NEXT', before a dozen words were uttered or a single verse of a song delivered, ended the dreams of many aspiring entertainers. Still, it is worth recording that by 1945, ENSA had given pleasure, of whatever degree, to audiences totalling over 500 million.

Post World War II, the administrative headache of Covent Garden had in no way abated. Spread over an area of some twnety acres, the Market handled over a million tons of fruit and vegetables every year. In the early 1950s a government committee was set up under the chairmanship of Lord Runciman 'to investigate the facilities and methods of marketing home-produced and imported vegetables, fruit and flowers; to consider whether the marketing and distribution of such produce can be improved; and to make recommendations'.

Published in 1957, The Runciman Report, was damning.

Just as Covent Garden is the biggest market in the country, so is the congestion around it the worst...at 6.30 a.m. on a typical market day as many as 1,500 vehicles, many of them heavy vehicles, may be stationary in the market area, and more than half of that number is likely still to be in the area by 10.30 a.m. The figures take no account of the moving vehicles and of the hand barrows used by market porters.

The Report added 'It is a tribute to the patience and skill of all concerned in market operations that the market manages to work at all'.

But Runciman fell short of recommending that the entire Market should be moved to a site outside central London. Such a move, it was argued, would have 'undesirable effects on marketing'. Instead:

Brentford and Stratford markets should be expanded and improved, and a new wholesale market should be created to serves the north-west of London, in order to reduce the volume of trade concentrated in Covent Garden.

Improvements should be made at Covent Garden Market to provide proper facilities for that market to perform its national functions.

A London Market Authority should be established.

A nod of approval from the government led to the creation of a Covent Garden Market Authority with powers under the Ministry of Agriculture to acquire by compulsory purchase all Market properties with a view to improve facilities while planning to re-build the Market 'either on the present site or on a new one within the Covent Garden area'. The necessary legislation entered the statute book in 1961.

Progress was slow. Over the next five years, the only noticeable improvement was the rationalisation of the labour market where, henceforth, the porters who did the lifting and carrying with in the Market, the pitchers who unloaded from incoming vehicles and warehousemen should all be known as porters operating under an employment regime that levelled up wages and limited the working hours to forty-four hours over five and a half days.

However beneficial to the workforce, there was no improvement in Market efficiency. Clemence Dane, who lived in the heart of the Market, noted in her book *London Has a Garden*, the chaos retained its charms.

An eccentricity is the Market habitués' complete disregard of traffic. The barrow-boys take precedence as a matter of course, and the morning buyers skitter across the narrow gaps between lorry and lorry like water-beetles crossing a pond, and the old hands who crouch in the gutter are hard to move as they furtively pick-over broken-stalked marguerites and wilted carnations. Later they wipe clean the faces of the flowers, scissor the petals, wipe the heads and make buttonholes out of their loot to sell at street-corners.

Other writers were drawn to what for them was the magic of Covent Garden. Here is the novelist and dramatist R.F. Delderfield on the 'City of Ordered Confusion':

Leicester Square quite deserted and London hardly stirring. Quiet, empty pavements as far as Charing Cross Road, and then? The first bastions of the City of Silent Uproar, the Stronghold of Stronger Language, the seething, sweating, swirling, searing centre of every grower's web. To boot, Covent Garden. 'Go early!' they tell you, but it is never early enough. You never see its heart begin to beat. By the time you have entered Long Acre and skirmished over the advanced sapheads of Henrietta Street and Bedford Street, you are alone in one of the last garrisons of the Cockney, hemmed in by haricots, penned in by peaches, cut off by cucumbers; a place where the scent of Herefordshire and the Lea Valley do valiant battle with

*the reek of exhaust; a square mile where the drab grey of
London stone is a mere backcloth for a far richer display
of colour than an international exhibition of still life
canvases could offer.*

*This is Covent Garden. This is the Clapham Junction
and the Crewe of half the tomatoes, cabbage, carrots and
cauliflowers grown in the British Isles...They [the people
of Covent Garden] are members of a tribe that has
somehow wandered away from the rest of us and built a
strictly private fortress in the streets between the Strand
and Holborn. Here they have always lived, speaking
their own language and practising their own customs.
One can be with them but never of them. One is either
born into their midst or remains outside of it, stupefied
and amazed at their applications to a calling that is
almost a cult...*

For most Londoners the charms were wearing thin and
Covent Garden had long since lost its Bohemian appeal. Tighter
licensing laws meant that pubs and supper rooms had to close at
appointed hours and thus could no longer offer an all-night service. One of the last of the Covent Garden night clubs, the Nell
Gwyn in Long Acre, fell on hard times between the wars. The Nell
Gwyn was run by Henry Foster 'a tall, stout, bearded man, with
an ingratiating smile, an eager desire to stimulate his guests, and
an absolutely debased palate – if one might judge from his selection of spirituous liquors which was served by his waiters'. 'There

was an air of mystery', said J.B.Booth, 'an atmosphere of suspicion, about the concern that was very depressing. The omnipresence of Foster himself – perpetually smiling, always calling waiters to remove empty glasses, and to hint by his manner that you were not doing your whole duty "for the good of the house" – increased the feeling.' When Foster died so too did the Nell Gwyn.

Of fonder memory were the characters who had made Covent Garden rather special. One such was the hairdresser and wigmaker, Willy Clarkson, who provided hair pieces for all the London shows. Dressed nattily in a style Charles Dickens would have recognised, Clarkson was short and fat with bandy legs who walked as if on a roll. He attended every first night, and owned the Duchess Theatre on Catherine Street, one of the smallest West End theatres with a proscenium arch. Designed on a tightly restricted site, the Duchess, with its charming Art Deco frontage, was built with the stalls below street level.

Clarkson's first place of work was on Wellington Street, though with the expansion of the business he moved his base to Wardour Street in Soho. For the most part, Clarkson was well-regarded during his lifetime, he even held a royal appointment as a hairdresser, but he had some unsavoury friends one of whom helped him submit a fraudulent insurance claim after a fire at his warehouse. At the time of his death in 1934, he was facing prosecution for a number of claims he had made on warehouse fires thought to have been started deliberately. But theatre critic James Agate, doyen of his tribe, remembered Willy with affection. 'There was never anybody quite like him, and London is the poorer for losing that dwarfish, lisping, fantastic agreeable old Moll with the red curls and dirty hands'.

Agate himself was an habitué with a fluctuating reputation. After a lengthy apprenticeship on the *Manchester Guardian* he moved to the *Sunday Times* in 1923 and remained there until his death in 1947. Convinced that, at its best, the theatre was a source of inspiration and enlightenment, he championed the work of Henrik Ibsen whose plays, when first presented, were widely condemned as a subversion of public morality.

Agate showed no mercy to frivolous and vacuous entertainments that appealed to matinee audiences in London for a day out. In particular, he had despised the 'inane habit known as the musical comedies', the staple diet of the Gaiety and several other theatres. He was equally averse to light comedies and farces. When having walked out of an 'uninteresting dramatic comedy', he was reproved by the playwright, Agate retorted that 'an experienced taster doesn't have to swallow a whole barrel of bridge-water to know what he's drinking'.

Agate's Covent Garden home (he changed address seventeen times during his time in London) was a flat in Grape Street where almost every resident in the block was homosexual including the staff, this at a time when sex between men was a criminal offence. Agate made no secret of his proclivities except when it came to associating with his fellow enthusiasts for Hackney show horses, the high-stepping breed capable of trotting at high speed. For this unlikely and expensive hobby, Agate dressed the part with a brown bowler hat and a long overcoat. As told by Sir Donald Sinden, a fine actor and unrivalled raconteur, there came the day when Agate invited to lunch at his flat the President of the All England Trotting Ponies Association, an archetypal old-school Brigadier.

After lunch was served by J.A.'s manservant they decided to go for a walk. Arriving in the lift at the ground floor J.A. realised he had left his walking stick behind, and, in a tone of masculine thunder, he asked the hall porter, 'Get through to my man and tell him to bring my stick'.

The porter picked up the house phone and, overheard by the Brigadier, President of the All England Trotting Ponies Association, said: 'Is that you Emma? She's forgotten her wand again'.

Another favourite Sinden story was of Agate's journey north in a chauffeur-driven car.

He started late for an appointment in the Midlands. Ahead lay a sleepy village astride a crossroad, with a thirty m.p.h. sign and the derestriction sign hardly a hundred yards apart. The driver started to brake, but Agate insisted that they keep moving. Sure enough hiding around the corner was a police motorcyclist who gave chase and flagged down the car. The policeman slowly got off his machine, removed his gauntlets which he placed on the saddle, and came over to the car and bent down to the open window. On seeing the driver his demeanour changed: 'Hello!', he said and, putting his head in the car, give the driver a smacking kiss right on the lips and added, 'Get going and don't get caught again'.

The car started off.

'Do you know him?' asked the astonished Agate.

'I can't remember his name, sir,' replied the chauffeur, 'but we were in the guards together'.

The debate on the future of the Market continued into the early 1960s when the Covent Garden Authority came out finally with a proposal that the entire Market should move to Nine Elms, on the south side of the Thames then a derelict area but with every prospect of regeneration. Government approval having been secured, a date was fixed for the migration. In 1974 Covent Garden Market, after three hundred years in the heart of London, found its new home three miles away in a district where once gardeners had cultivated the land for produce to sell outside the wall of Bedford House.

Divested of its Market, what was to happen to Covent Garden? The Greater London Authority (successor to the London County Council) had in mind a massive redevelopment programme requiring the destruction of Maiden Lane, most of Henrietta Street, Drury Lane and St Martin's Lane, not to mention the relocation of thousands of residents. The aim was to create 'a new twentieth-century town community, recapturing the spirit of London's 18th century squares'. That sounded good in principle but doubts set in after 1968 when a first draft plan revealed an open space for some four acres straddling Long Acre with an adjoining sports centre, a conference centre in one corner of the Piazza (how planners loved their conference venues!) and new hotels on prime sites. Among the conservationists what really set the alarm bells ringing was the proposal to build roads to carry heavy traffic through the area. Though partly to be sunk below ground, it did not take much imagination to visualise the impact of four-lane motorways on the local community, not to mention tourists and other visitors. It was small comfort to know that pedestrians would have their own walkways free of cars but, as it appeared, free of anything that was eye-catchingly attractive.

Led by a brilliantly organised campaign by Covent Garden residents and businesses, a public backlash forced the government to step in with a demand for a new plan to be prepared with 'full public participation'. The result was the preservation of nearly all that was best of the old Market and the regeneration of a centre that is attractive, exciting and commercially viable; the Covent Garden of today.

Selected Bibliography

Peter Ackroyd, *Dickens*, 1990

James Agate, *Ego, 9 volumes*, 1935-1946

Gilbert Armitage, *The History of the Bow Street Runners*, 1932

Brenda Assael, *The London Restaurant, 1840-1914*, 2018

Nina Auerbach, *Ellen Terry, Player in her Time*, 1987

Felix Barker, *The House that Stoll Built*, 1957

J M Beattie, *The First English Detectives: The Bow Street Runners and the Policing of London, 1750-1840*, 2012

Karl Beckson, *London in the 1890s: A Cultural History*, 1992

Madeline Bingham, *Henry Irving and the Victorian Theatre*, 1978

J B Booth, *London Town*, 1929; *The Days We Knew* 1943; *Palmy Days* 1957

E J Burford, *Wits, Wenches and Wantons*, 1986

E Beresford Chancellor, *The Private Palaces of London: Past and Present*, 1908

M Clifton, *Manuel de la Conversation et du Style Epistolaire, Français-Anglais*, 1877

Jonathan Conlin, *Tales of Two Cities: Paris, London and the Birth of the Modern City*, 2013

Gordon Craig, *Henry Irving*, 1930

Clemence Dane, *London has a Garden*, 1964

Alan Dent, *My Covent Garden*, 1973

M Willson Disher, *Winkles and Champagne*, 1938

Raymond Fitzsimons, *Edmund Kean, Fire from Heaven*, 1976

Ring In the New

G Laurence Gomme, *London in the Reign of Victoria 1837-1897*, 1898

John Hollingshead, *Plain English*, 1880

Adam Hyman, *The Gaiety Years*, 1975

Laurence Irving, *Henry Irving: The Actor and his World*, 1951

Lee Jackson, *Palaces of Pleasure*, 2019

Joan Lock, *Tales from Bow Street*, 1982

Ian McIntyre, *Garrick*, 1999

J Holden MacMichael, *The Story of Charing Cross and Its Immediate Neighbour-hood*, 1906

Ann Monsarrat, *An Uneasy Victorian: Thackeray the Man, 1811-1863*, 1980

Franny Moyle, *Turner: The Extraordinary Life and Momentous Times of J M W Turner*, 2016

Donald Olsen, *The Growth of Victorian London*, 1976

W Macqueen-Pope, *Twenty Shillings in the Pound*, 1948; *Theatre Royal, Drury Lane*, 1945

Lieut-Col Newnham-Davis, *Dinners and Diners: Where and How to Dine in London*, 1899

Roy Porter, *London: A Social History*, 1994

Joanna Richardson, *The Courtesans*, 1967

John Richardson, *Covent Garden Past*, 1995

William Robson, *The Government and Misgovernment of London*, 1939

Hallie Rubenhold, *The Covent Garden Ladies*, 2005

Andrew Saint, *London 1870-1914, A City at its Zenith*, 2021

Max Schlesinger, *Saunterings In and About London*, 1853

Harold Scott, *The Early Doors: Origins of the Music Hall*, 1946

Desmond Shawe-Taylor, *Covent Garden*, 1948

George Speaight, *Punch & Judy: A History*, 1970

Gavin Stamp, *Interwar British Architecture 1919-39*, 2024

Robert Thorne, *Covent Garden Market*, 1980

Barry Turner, *Men of Letters: The Story of Garrick Writers*, 2019

Warren Tute, *The Grey Top Hat: The Story of Moss Bros*, 1961

John Wain, *The Journals of James Boswell, 1762-1795*, 1991

Covent Garden and Strand

Maureen Waller, *1700: Scenes from London Life*, 2000

Geoffrey Wansell, *The Garrick: Story of a Club*, 2013

Paul Webb, *Ivor Novello: Portrait of a Star*, 1999

Ronald Webber, *Covent Garden: Mud-Salad Market*, 1969

Roger Wilmot, *Kindly Leave the Stage*, 1985

A E Wilson, *The Lyceum*, 1952

Frances Wilson, *Guilty Thing: A Life of Thomas De Quincey*, 2016

Horace Wyndham, Chorus to Coronet, 1951

Acknowledgements

Above all others, I must thank my wife, Mary Fulton, for her active participation in the research and for editing the book into a manageable shape.

As always, the London Library, with its highly professional and helpful staff, has proved to be a treasure house of source material.

Privileged to draw on the resources of the Garrick Club, I owe thanks to Professor Robin Simon, Chairman of the Works of Art committee, and to Trustee and Club historian, Geoffrey Wansell.

My publisher Richard Charkin, who crowned his illustrious career by founding Mensch Publishing, has given me all the helpful attention any author could desire.

Any errors that have crept in must be taken squarely upon my chin alone.

I dedicate this book to my young grandchildren, Eve, Freya, Max, Leo and Aksel in the hope that their London will prove to be a voyage of exciting discovery.

A Note on the Author

Barry Turner is an author, editor and reviewer. He has written over thirty books, most recently *Piccadilly: The Story of the World's Most Famous Thoroughfare* also published by Mensch Publishing. Other titles include *Men of Letters: The Story of Garrick Writers; Thorns in the Crown: the Story of the Coronation* and *Waiting for War: Britain 1939-1940*. He is also the author of *The Berlin Airlift; Beacon For Change: How the 1951 Festival of Britain Shaped the Modern Age* and of *Suez 1956*. He has contributed to newspapers including *The Times* and *The Sunday* Times and currently reviews classic crime novels for the *Daily Mail*. Barry lives in London and south-west France.